The Complete
Rock & Pop
Guitar Player
Omnibus Edition

D0552187

WISE PUBLICATIONS
London / New York / Paris / Sydney / Copenhagen / Berlin / Madrid / Tokyo

PART 1

PART 2

PART 3

Published by
Wise Publications
8/9 Frith Street, London W1D 3JB

Exclusive Distributors:
Music Sales Limited,
Distribution Centre, Newmarket Road,
Bury St Edmunds, Suffolk IP33 3YB, England
Music Sales Pty Limited,
120 Rothschild Avenue, Rosebery,
NSW 2018, Australia

Order No. AM977339
ISBN 1-84449-050-5
This book © Copyright 2004 by Wise Publications

Written and arranged by Rikky Rooksby.
Music Processed by Paul Ewers.
Edited by Sorcha Armstrong.

Cover & book design by Fresh Lemon.
Cover photograph by George Taylor.
Artist photographs courtesy of
London Features International/ Redferns.

CD mastered by Jonas Persson.
Guitars by Arthur Dick.
Programming by John Moores and Chris Norton.

Printed in Malta by Interprint Limited.

Your Guarantee of Quality:
As publishers, we strive to produce every book to the
highest commercial standards. This book has been carefully
designed to minimise awkward page turns and to make
playing from it a real pleasure. Particular care has been
given to specifying acid-free, neutral-sized paper made from
pulps which have not been elemental chlorine bleached.
This pulp is from farmed sustainable forests and was
produced with special regard for the environment.
Throughout, the printing and binding have been planned
to ensure a sturdy, attractive publication which should give
years of enjoyment. If your copy fails to meet our high
standards, please inform us and we will gladly replace it.

www.musicsales.com

GOT ANY COMMENTS?
Email: completerockandpop@musicsales.co.uk

The Complete Rock & Pop Guitar Player
Part 1

INTRODUCTION

Welcome to *The Complete Rock & Pop Guitar Player Part 1*. This is the first in a three-part course which can help you to play rock and pop guitar.

From the beginning this book teaches you to play classic songs, faster than you thought possible. Just three chords and you can play along with tracks like '**No Woman, No Cry**', '**Common People**' and '**Brimful Of Asha**'. You learn to play simply by following the easy strum patterns and chords written above the lyrics. You don't even have to read any music!

The songs are carefully graded, each one adding a new chord, a new strum pattern, or other technique.

By the time you have finished Part 1 you will have learnt over 20 basic chords and many useful strum patterns. You will be ready to move on to more chords, strumming techniques, and some single note playing in Parts 2 and 3.

Everything is made really simple for you. All the musical examples are recorded on the CD for Part 1, first with the guitar demonstration version, and then without it as a backing track for you to play along with.

THE GUITAR

To play the songs in this book you can use a nylon-strung 'classical' guitar, a steel-strung acoustic, or an electric guitar. Of these the nylon-strung guitar is not so effective for strumming. Its nylon strings won't produce quite as good a sound for rhythm guitar as steel strings. Nylon strings sound better with finger-style pieces.

Whether you have an acoustic or an electric guitar, the principles of playing are fundamentally the same, and so are most of the features on both instruments.

ACOUSTIC GUITAR

ELECTRIC GUITAR

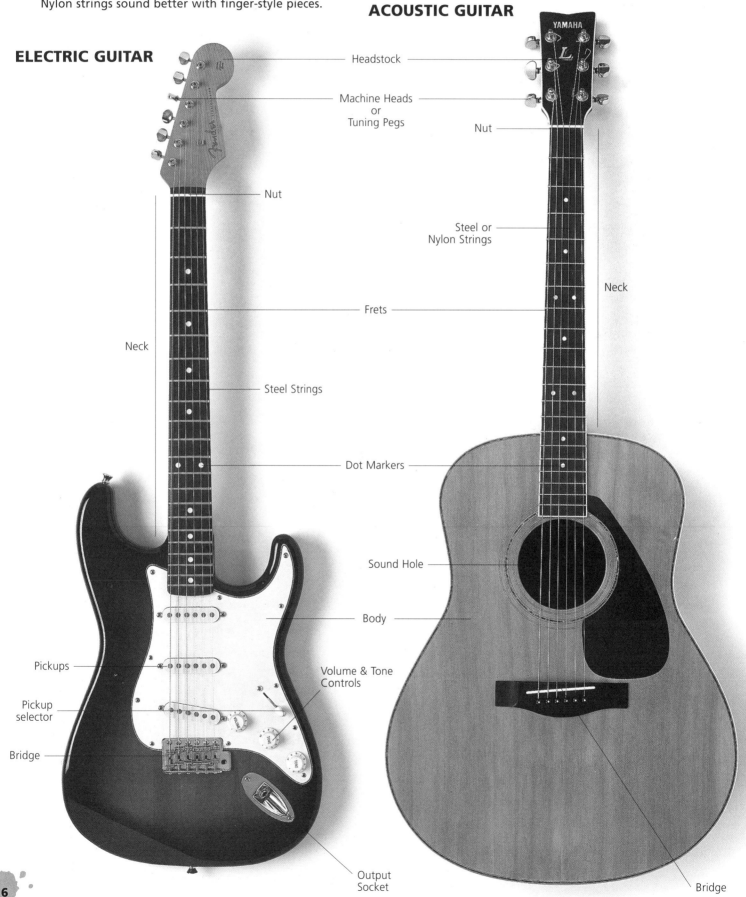

Headstock

Machine Heads
or
Tuning Pegs

Nut

Nut

Steel or
Nylon Strings

Neck

Neck

Frets

Steel Strings

Dot Markers

Sound Hole

Body

Pickups

Volume & Tone
Controls

Pickup
selector

Bridge

Output
Socket

Bridge

PLAYING THE GUITAR

The picture left shows a comfortable position for playing guitar.

THE RIGHT OR STRUMMING HAND

When strumming it is desirable to use a pick or plectrum. You can use your thumb, or brush the strings with the nail-side of your fingers held together. However, a pick produces a more defined and clear sound. If you're left-handed, you should use your left hand for strumming, and your right hand for fretting.

THE LEFT OR FRETTING HAND

Use your finger tips to press down the strings in the positions described in this book. Your thumb should be behind your 1st and 2nd fingers pressing on the middle of the back of the neck. It should retain its natural curve. In other words, don't bend it at the centre thumb joint. Keep the thumb vertical. Never allow the flat of the palm of your fretting hand to touch the neck. The only point of contact should be where the neck is cradled in the skin that runs from your index finger along the edge of the hand and up to your thumb.

If you are left-handed, the fretting hand will be your right hand, and the strumming hand will be your left.

THE PLECTRUM

Picks come in many sizes, shapes and thicknesses, and are available from your local music shop. The larger ones are easier to keep hold of, and for strumming you want one of the thinner types because these put up less resistance to the strings. The photo shows the correct way to hold your plectrum. Generally speaking the thumb crosses behind the tip of the index finger at roughly a right angle to grip the pick.

TUNING

Accurate tuning of the guitar is essential and is achieved by winding the machine heads up or down. It is always better to tune 'up' to the correct pitch rather than down. Therefore, if you find that the pitch of your string is higher (sharper) than the correct pitch, you should 'wind' down below the correct pitch and *then* tune up to it.

RELATIVE TUNING

Relative tuning simply means tuning the guitar to itself without the aid of a pitch pipe or other tuning device. Here's how to do it:

Estimate the pitch of the 6th string as near as possible to E, or at least a comfortable pitch (not too high, as you might break other strings when tuning up).
Then, while checking the various positions on the diagram above, place a finger from your fretting hand on:

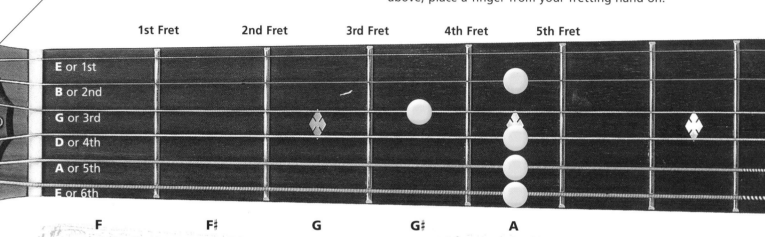

Head

The 5th fret of the 6th string **E** and **tune the 5th string A** to the note produced **A**

The 5th fret of the 5th string **A** and **tune the 4th string D** to the note **D**

The 5th fret of the 4th string **D** and **tune the 3rd string G** to the note **G**

The 4th fret of the 3rd string **G** and **tune the 2nd string B** to the note **B**

The 5th fret of the 2nd string **B** and **tune the 1st string E** to the note **E**

This is the most commonly used system for relative tuning. It's more accurate if you use a tuning fork, pitch pipe, piano or track 1 on the CD to find the pitch of the sixth string **E**. However, all of the notes are given on our CD on track 1, as a handy reference guide.

OTHER METHODS OF TUNING

Other ways to tune your guitar include using pitch pipes, tuning fork or an electronic tuner. These are all available from music shops.

CHORD BOXES

Chord boxes are diagrams of the guitar neck viewed head upwards, face on, as illustrated in the diagram above. The horizontal double line at the top represents the nut, and the other horizontal lines are the frets. The vertical lines are the strings, starting from the 6th **E** on the left, to the 1st **top E** on the right.

Any dots with numbers inside them simply indicate which finger goes where. Any strings marked with an **X** must not be played; strings marked with an **O** are played open.

The fingers of your fretting hand are numbered **1**, **2**, **3** & **4** as on the photo below.

YOUR FIRST CHORD
The **C** chord.

Remember:

X Don't Play String

O Play Open String

C Chord

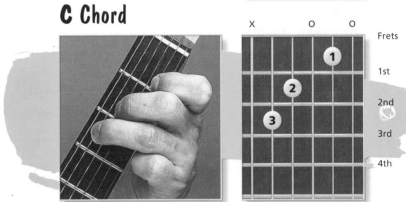

LEFT (OR FRETTING) HAND
Place all three fingers into position and press down firmly, just behind the metal fret wire. Keep your thumb near the middle of the back of the neck, behind your **2nd** finger.

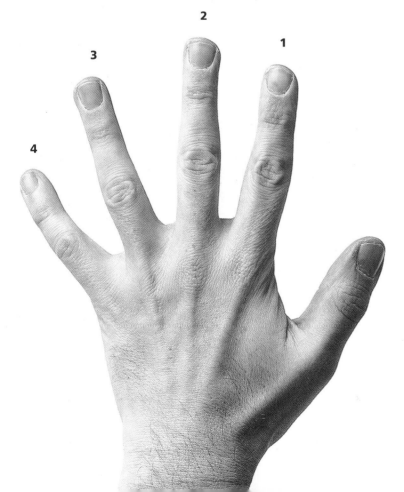

RIGHT HAND THUMB OR PLECTRUM
Slowly play each string in the chord, starting with the 5th **A** string – notice that the bottom string has an **X** over it – and moving up to the 1st **E** string. If there is any buzzing, maybe you need to:
- **Position your fingers nearer the metal fret (towards you)**
- **Adjust the angle of your hand**
- **Check that the buzz is not elsewhere on the guitar by playing the open strings in the same way.**

Once you have a 'buzz free' sound, play the chord a few times and then remove your fingers and repeat the exercise until your positioning is right instinctively.

USING A CAPO
Sometimes you will need to use a capo in order to play along with the songs in this book.

A capo is simply a small device that clamps across the guitar neck, to raise the pitch of all the strings together – making it useful when transposing songs or simplifying chords. They come in different forms, from cheap, basic ones, to more sturdy types. You can get one from any guitar shop – it might be the most useful accessory you ever buy!

PAPERBACK WRITER
Words & Music by John Lennon & Paul McCartney

G Chord

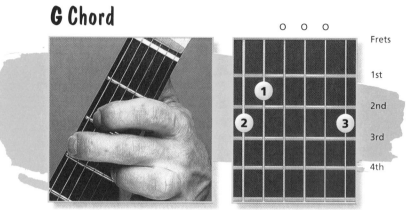

To play this Beatles classic you need just two chords. Place your fingers in the correct positions and press down firmly. Remember to keep your thumb around the middle back of the neck and behind your 1st and 2nd fingers. Then follow the same procedure as you did for the C chord, this time starting with the 6th E string.

Check that all the strings are sounding cleanly by playing them one at a time. Then play the whole chord with a downstroke of your hand or pick.

Holding down the G chord try strumming this rhythm using down strokes. These are signified by a downward arrow. Try to keep your strums evenly spaced.

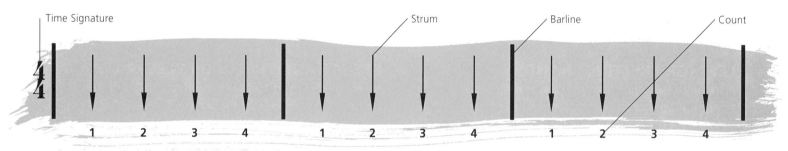

Well, if you want to sound technical you can say you have just played your first three bars of **4/4** time. Basically, **4/4** (four-four) time means four beats in a bar. These bars are separated by a bar-line which means the end of one bar and the beginning of another.

Now, still holding down your **G** chord, practise changing to **C** with your 'four in a bar' rhythm, this time accentuating the first strum of every bar. It is best to play slowly and evenly at first, so that you have time to change chords without stopping.

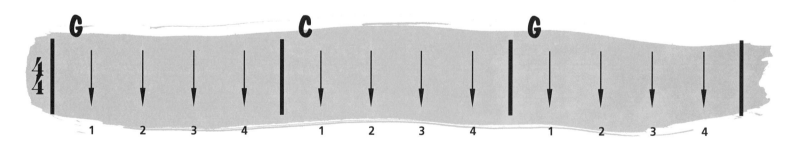

There is another way of fingering a **G** chord. By playing it with your **2nd**, **3rd** and **4th** fingers you make it easier to change to **C** because your 1st finger is ready to go down on the 1st fret of the 2nd string, and the 2nd and 3rd fingers can keep their shape but just move across a string.

'Paperback Writer' has quite a fast tempo - but don't worry! You don't have to strum fast in this version. All you need to do is play downward on the chord on each first and third beat. The introduction consists of two bars of 'clicks' followed by four bars of the famous guitar riff. Listen to the demonstration on **Track 2**, then try it by yourself with **Track 3**. Don't rush ahead to the next song until you're confident with this one.

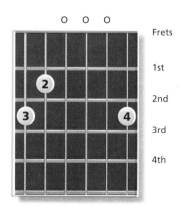

2 BAR CLICK INTRO

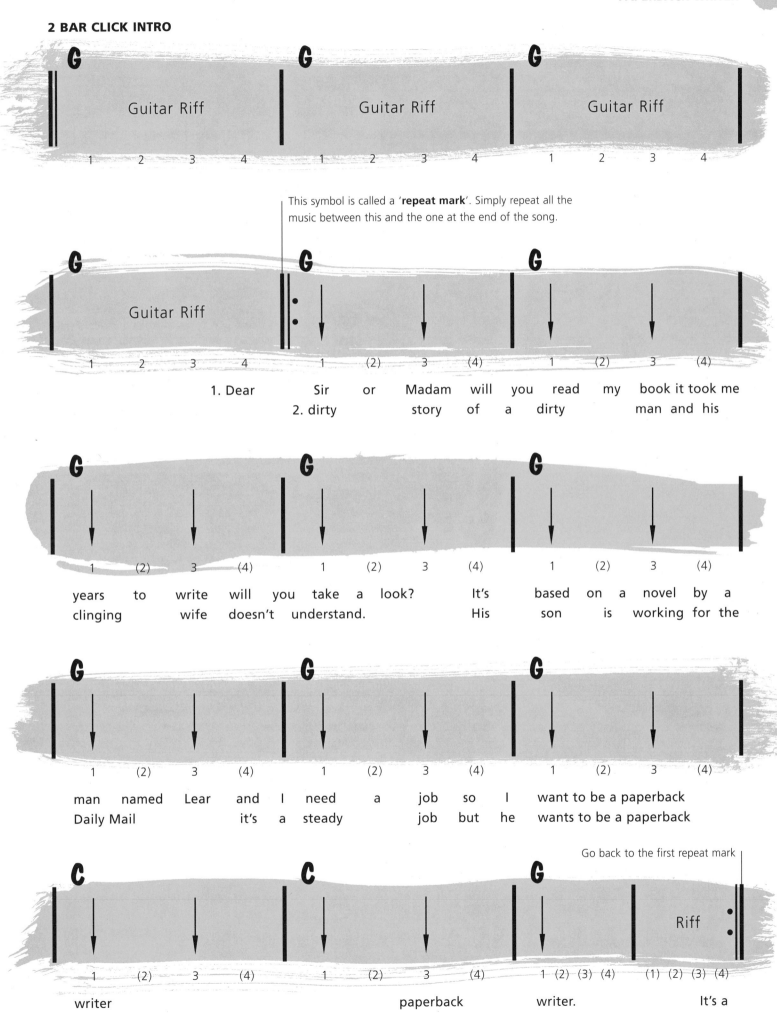

This symbol is called a '**repeat mark**'. Simply repeat all the music between this and the one at the end of the song.

1. Dear Sir or Madam will you read my book it took me
2. dirty story of a dirty man and his

years to write will you take a look? It's based on a novel by a
clinging wife doesn't understand. His son is working for the

man named Lear and I need a job so I want to be a paperback
Daily Mail it's a steady job but he wants to be a paperback

Go back to the first repeat mark

writer paperback writer. It's a

BRIMFUL OF ASHA
Words & Music by Tjinder Singh

After an unsuccessful release in 1997, this song was re-mixed and re-released in 1998, making it to No. 1! You're going to learn the album version here.

D Chord

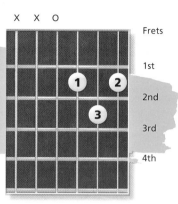

Now it's time for you to learn your second tune, a No.1 hit for Corner Shop in 1998, 'Brimful Of Asha'. We're going to learn one new chord and one new strumming pattern. The song has three basic parts - the verse, the chorus and the bridge - and uses G, C and D.

D major is played from the 4th string, which is **D**, the root note of the chord. When you strum it try to avoid hitting the 6th and 5th strings.

Instead of just strumming down on each beat, we will strum down *and up* on each beat. If you look at the first bar you'll see 1&2& etc. written under the words. Tap your foot four times in each bar and on the first tap count '1&', on the second tap '2&' and so on. The number is the downstroke and the '&' is the upstroke. Upstrokes may seem a little strange at first but you will soon get accustomed to them. You will notice the benefit of strumming with a soft pick when you do upstrokes.

The original version is in **A major**, as is the backing CD. Since **A major** is one tone (two frets) higher than **G major**, all you have to do is put a capo on the second fret of the guitar and use the **G**, **C** and **D** shapes. After you learn the chords for **A** and **E** you can come back and try playing 'Brimful' without the capo to compare the sound. (Without a capo, for a **G** play **A**, for **C** play **D** and for **D** play **E**).

CAPO 2ND FRET
8 BAR INTRO

Look out for the repeat marks!

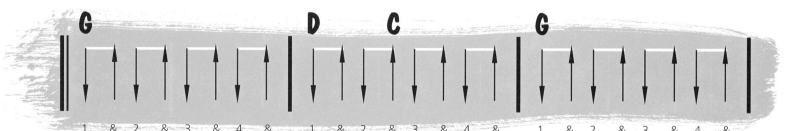

G	D	C	G
1 & 2 & 3 & 4 &	1 & 2 & 3 & 4 &		1 & 2 & 3 & 4 &

There's dancing   be – hind movie scenes behind the   movie scenes

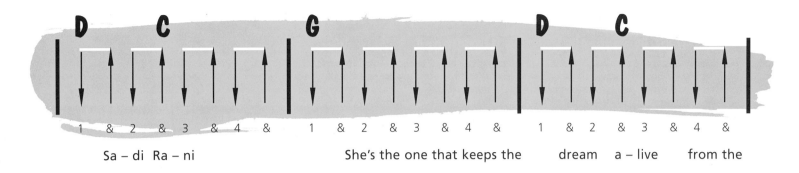

Sa – di Ra – ni   She's the one that keeps the   dream a – live   from the

CHORUS

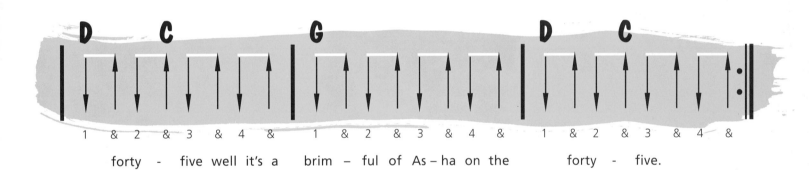

morning past the evening to the   end of the   light.   Brim – ful of As – ha on the

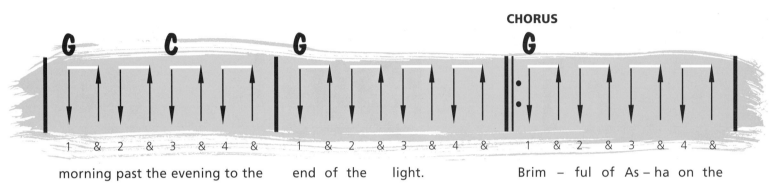

forty - five well it's a   brim – ful of As – ha on the   forty - five.

BRIDGE

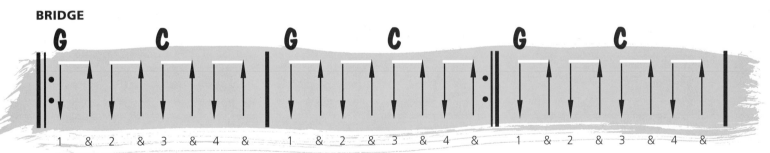

Everybody needs a bosom for a pillow   everybody needs a bosom.   Everybody needs a bosom for a pillow

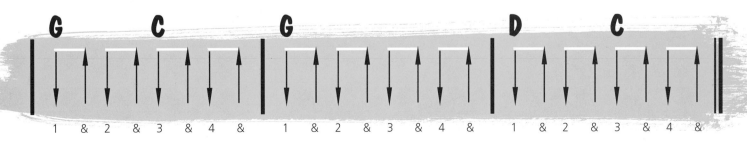

everybody needs a bosom, mine's on the forty-five.

HELLO, I LOVE YOU
Words & Music by Jim Morrison, Robbie Krieger, Ray Manzarek & John Densmore

A Chord

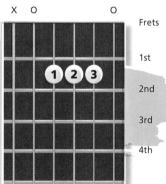

'Hello I Love You' was a No.1 in 1968 for The Doors, featuring the great Jim Morrison on vocals. You can find it on their *Strange Days* album. It requires one new chord, A major, played from the 5th string, which is A, the root of the chord.

Start by placing your 1st finger on the 2nd fret of the 4th string and then locate the other finger positions. If you find it a problem squeezing all three fingers into the space, you can always try using the 2nd, 3rd and 4th (so that the 4th is on the 2nd string).

The strum pattern is the same for '**Brimful Of Asha**', down and up on each beat. Each of these strums represents the rhythm value of an 8th note. So we can call this a strum in straight 8ths.

Notice that when you change from **D** to **A** your 3rd finger does not need to lift off the 2nd string; it only needs to move back or forward one fret. This is called a 'guide finger'. Spotting a guide finger - a finger that moves along a string and therefore does not have to lift off - will help you change chord faster.

Apparently, The Doors got their name from the Aldous Huxley text "all the other chemical doors in the wall are labelled Dope....". We're enlightened!

4 BAR INTRO

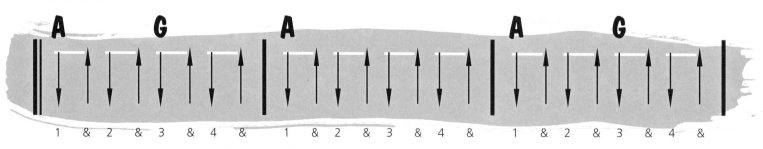

A		G		A				A		G	
1	&	2	&	3	&	4	&	1	&	2	&	3	&	4	&	1	&	2	&	3	&	4	&

Hel – lo,   I love you won't you   tell me your name.   Hel – lo,   I love you let me

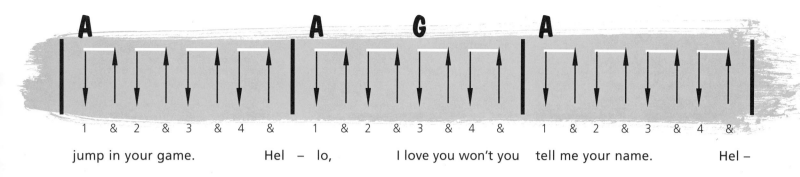

jump in your game.   Hel – lo,   I love you won't you   tell me your name.   Hel –

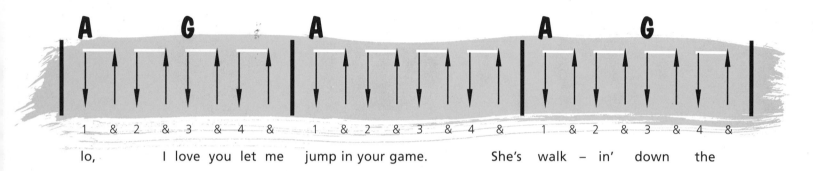

lo,   I love you let me   jump in your game.   She's walk – in' down the

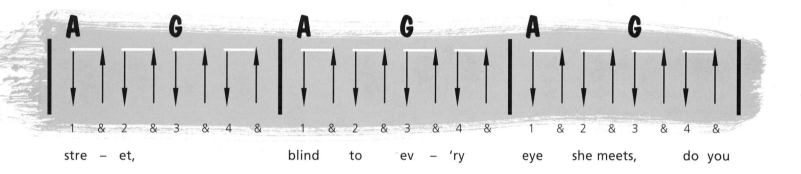

stre – et,   blind to ev – 'ry   eye she meets,   do you

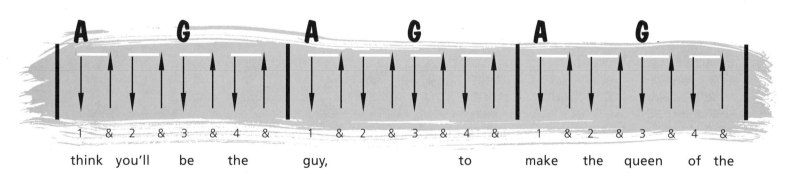

think you'll be the   guy,   to make the queen of the

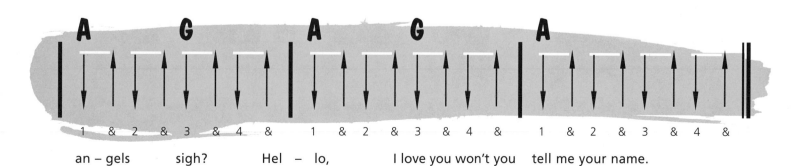

an – gels   sigh?   Hel – lo,   I love you won't you   tell me your name.

ROCK AROUND THE CLOCK
Words & Music by Max C. Freedman & Jimmy De Knight

Bill Haley and His Comets' 'Rock Around The Clock' helped start a revolution in popular music in 1955. Featured in the film *Blackboard Jungle*, it sold millions worldwide and turned people on to rock'n'roll.

E Chord

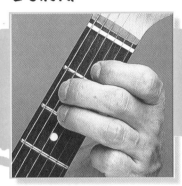

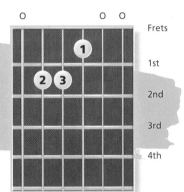

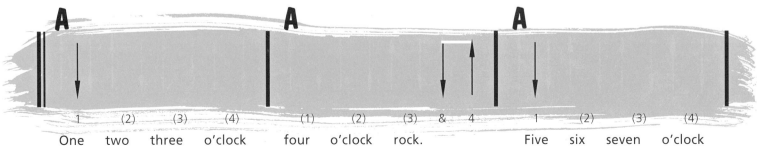

This song spent 8 weeks at No.1 and was the most successful Rock'n'Roll record of all time!

Many rock'n'roll songs use a verse structure called a 'twelve-bar', taken from the blues but played at a quicker tempo. If you count the bars from the start of the verse you will find '**Rock Around The Clock**' has twelve bars and just three chords. Yes, it's **A**, **D** and a new chord, **E**.

E major is a significant chord on the guitar. Easy to play, it allows you to hit all six strings and to have the open 6th string - the guitar's lowest note - sounding. No other major chord on the guitar sounds quite like **E**!

For the intro only strike the chords on the beats marked. There are gaps where there is only the voice. As '**Rock Around The Clock**' is fast, we are going to use a single (1/4 note) strum to each beat, with occasional up-strokes on the third off-beats (in time with the snare-drum).

When you get confident with the chord changes you can experiment with strumming 8ths, down and up on each beat. However, because the song uses a 'swung' rhythm it is as if the beat is divided into three rather than two. Instead of straight 8ths, where the two strums are rhythmically equal, in a 'swung rhythm' song the first strum is twice as long as the second. Tap your foot in a steady 4/4 time and say 1 2 3 on each beat instead of 1 &. Your first strum will be down on '1' and up on '3'. Practise this slowly at first.

2 BAR INTRO ♫ = ♩♪ This means 'swing rhythm'

A				A				A			
1	(2)	(3)	(4)	(1)	(2)	(3)	& 4	1	(2)	(3)	(4)
One	two	three	o'clock	four	o'clock	rock.		Five	six	seven	o'clock

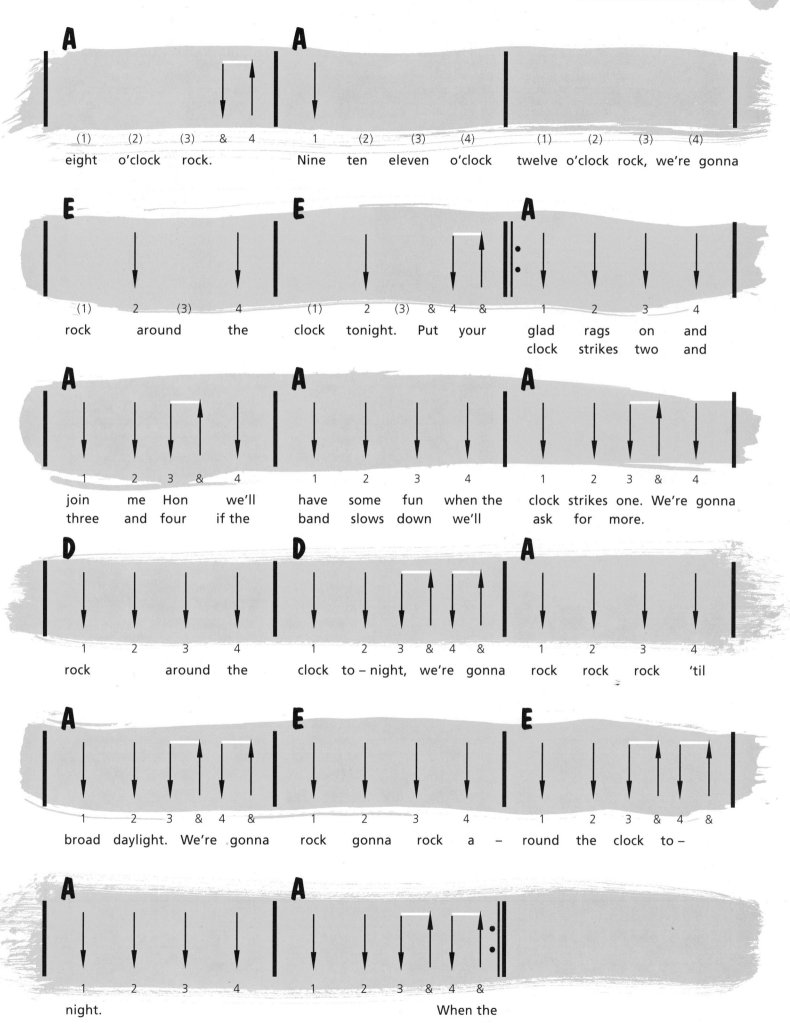

THAT'LL BE THE DAY
Words & Music by Buddy Holly, Norman Petty & Jerry Allison

B7 Chord

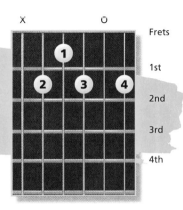

Frets
1st
2nd
3rd
4th

This song was the title song to the 1970's movie That'll Be The Day.

One new chord is needed for this rock'n'roll standard from Buddy Holly and the Crickets, a No.1 in 1957.

B7 is actually easier to play than a straight **B major** chord, even though it is slightly more complex.

Like '**Rock Around The Clock**', '**That'll Be The Day**' has a swing feel, so when you strum the 8ths they are not equal pairs. Each downstroke on the beat lasts roughly twice as long as the upstroke on the offbeat.

Listen carefully to the demonstration (**Track 10**) to get the feel of this rhythm.

Take a look at bar 7. You'll notice only one arrow in the bar. What this means is that you should play the first beat only, then mute the strings while you count '2, 3, 4'. In the next bar, you'll see that there is no down arrow on the first beat of the bar. This means that you don't play bar 1, but instead start strumming on the '&' with an upstroke.

Watch out also for the last bar – here you strum three times on each beat. Three notes played in the time of one are called triplets. Again, listen to the demonstration to hear how this should be played.

2 BAR INTRO

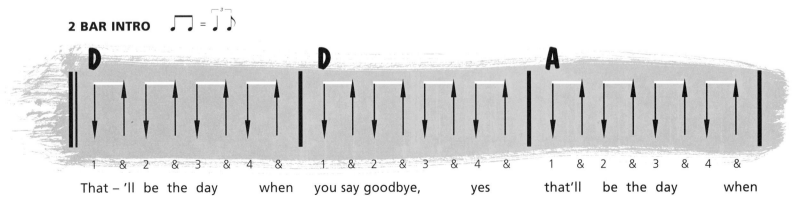

	1	&	2	&	3	&	4	&	1	&	2	&	3	&	4	&	1	&	2	&	3	&	4	&
	That –	'll	be	the	day		when		you	say	goodbye,		yes				that'll		be	the	day		when	

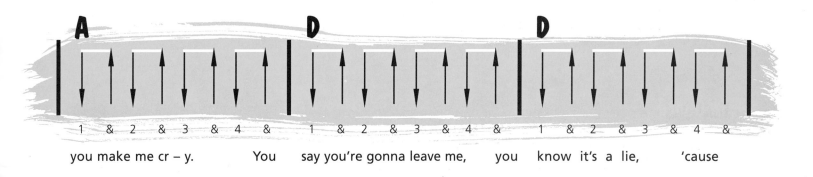

you make me cr – y.   You   say you're gonna leave me,   you   know it's a lie,   'cause

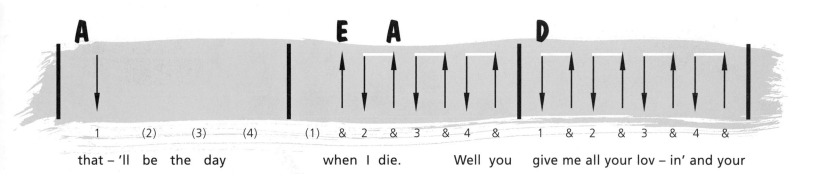

that – 'll be the day   when I die.   Well you   give me all your lov – in' and your

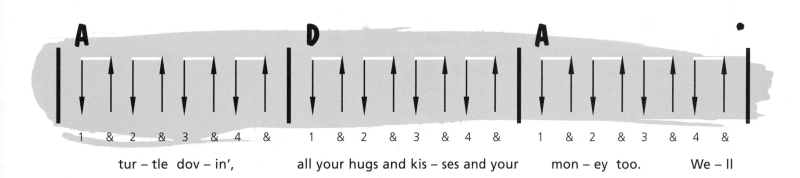

tur – tle dov – in',   all your hugs and kis – ses and your   mon – ey too.   We – ll

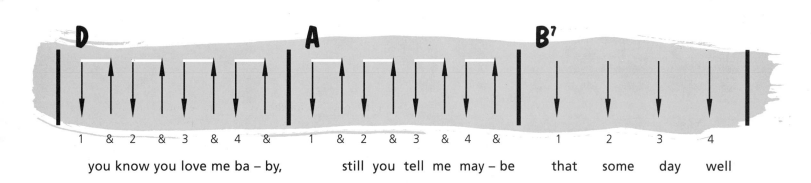

you know you love me ba – by,   still you tell me may – be   that   some   day   well

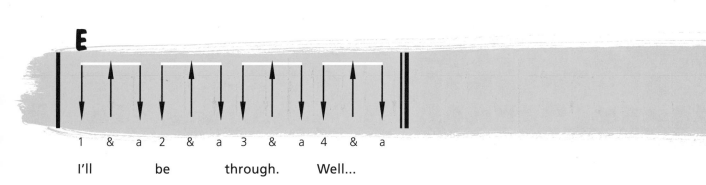

I'll   be   through.   Well...

I WANNA BE ADORED

Words & Music by John Squire & Ian Brown

Em Chord

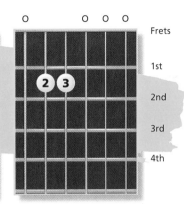

Frets
1st
2nd
3rd
4th

This track was released in 1991 and features John Squire at his best... big atmospheric catchy riffs.

This atmospheric track by The Stone Roses is one of the stand-out songs of their 1989 debut album. There is one new chord for this song, E minor.

Like **E major**, **E minor** is effective because it uses all six strings and the lowest note on the guitar. This gives **E minor** its characteristic deep, resonant tone. If you compare it with **E** (by putting your first finger on the **1st fret** of the **3rd string**), you can hear the difference in tone. In contrast with major chords, minor chords sound sad.

'**I Wanna Be Adored**' gives us the opportunity to experiment with a new strumming pattern.

The original track begins with a long instrumental passage featuring a strong 'chugging' 8th note rhythm. You could play the whole song in this way, with straight 8th notes (as in the first two bars). However, to make things a little more interesting, let's try the pattern in bars three and four. This pattern uses ties – see page 87. Break it down by counting really slowly: 1 2 3 & 4 & (1) & 2 & (3) & 4 &. Count, but don't play, the numbers in brackets – they are there to help you keep your place.

This is the first really challenging rhythm you've had, so take your time and get it right! The song starts with a four-bar fade in.

4 BAR FADE IN

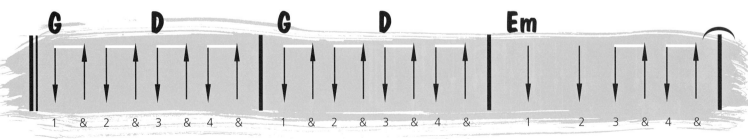

G				D				G				D				Em							
1	&	2	&	3	&	4	&	1	&	2	&	3	&	4	&	1		2	3	&	4	&	

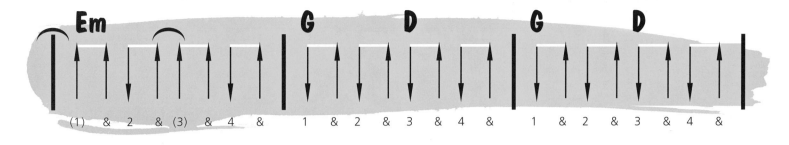

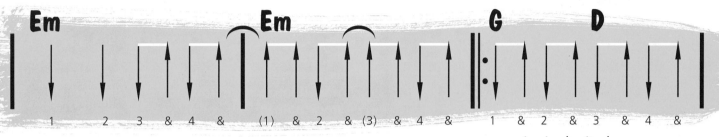

1. I don't have
2. I don't need

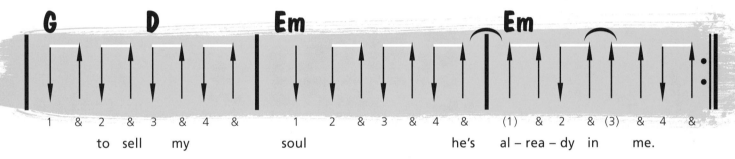

to sell my soul he's al – rea – dy in me.

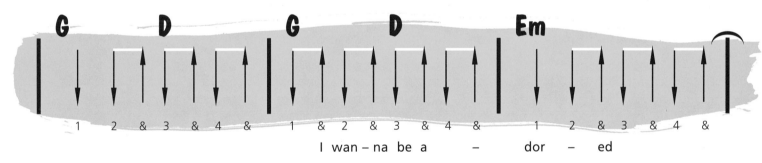

I wan – na be a – dor – ed

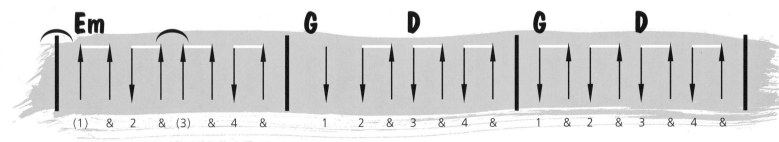

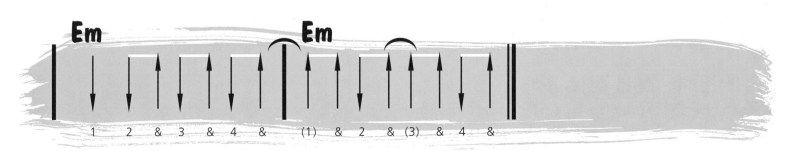

STAND BY ME
Words & Music by Ben E. King, Jerry Leiber & Mike Stoller

John Lennon's classic 1975 version was the last of several collaborations with the legendary producer and eccentric inventor of the 'Wall Of Sound', Phil Spector.

Let's use the same four chords for another song. 'Stand By Me' has been released by a number of artists and has been featured in many film and ad campaigns. Ben E. King had a hit with it in 1961 and in 1987 it was featured in a Levi's TV ad. In between, in 1975 John Lennon released a well-known version from his album *Rock'n'Roll*.

Up to now we have had a maximum of two strums per beat and we have been counting 1 & 2 & 3 & 4 & for each bar. If you look at the first beat of each bar you will see there is an extra strum between the '&' sign and the '2'. Count this extra strum as an 'a'.

So, the rhythm of each bar is counted like this: 1 &-a-2 & 3 & 4 &. Remember, you must arrive at the '2' on the second foot tap so you have to squeeze the 'a' strum in between the '&' and the '2'. The extra strum is pretty fast, so practise it slowly first.

Our recording features the full introduction, which is eight bars of music, plus two bars of click – 10 bars in total. Listen to the intro and see if you can tell when to come in – if not, our guitar demo will show you. Learning to count 'empty bars' (i.e. bars you aren't playing in) is a valuable skill.

CAPO 2ND FRET
8 BAR INTRO

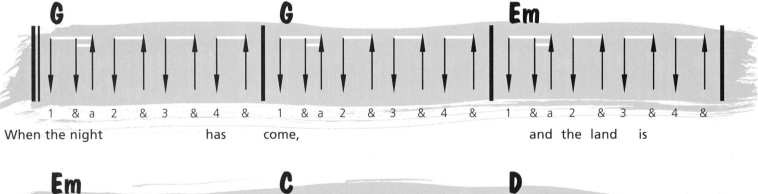

When the night   has   come,   and the land   is

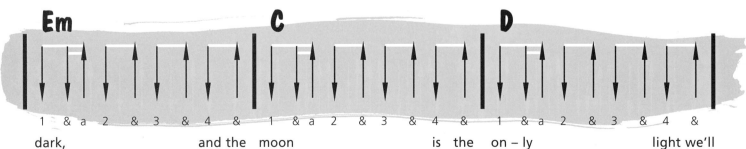

dark,   and the moon   is the on – ly   light we'll

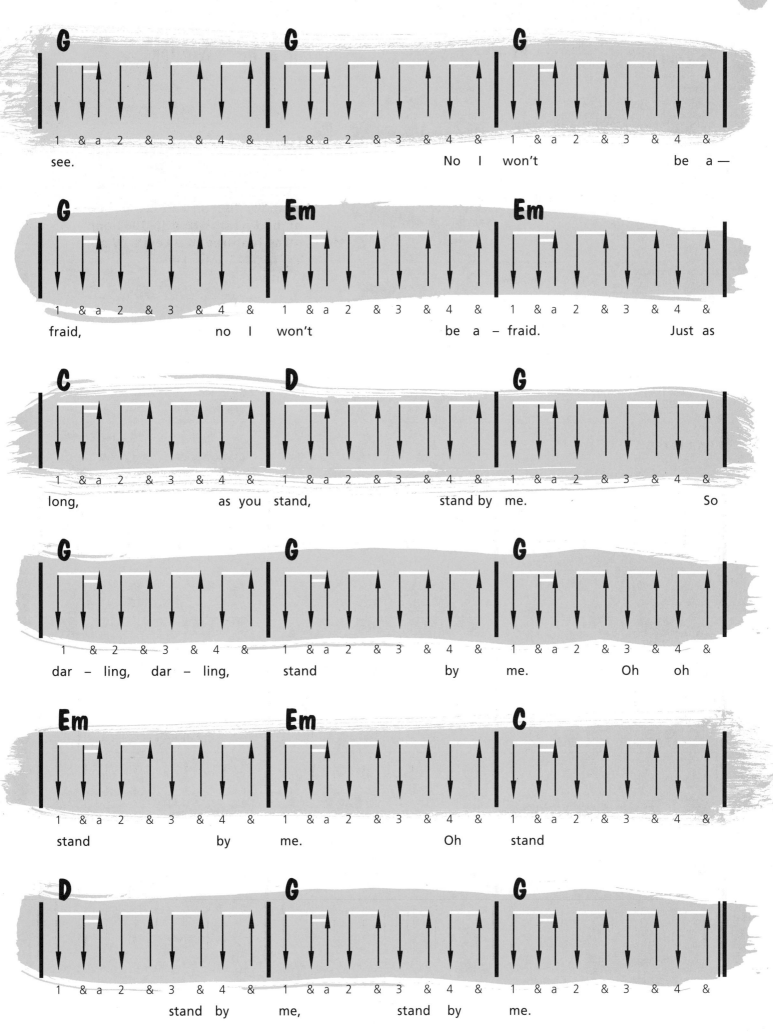

CATHY'S CLOWN
Words & Music by Don Everly

If you have a friend who can sing harmony now is the time to call them up! The next song is a classic of two-voice singing - The Everly Brothers' 'Cathy's Clown', which went to No.1. on both sides of the Atlantic in 1960.

Surprisingly, given the very different themes of the songs, it uses the same chords - **G**, **C**, **D** and **Em** - as '**I Wanna Be Adored**' and '**Stand By Me**'.

The strumming is quite easy. During the chorus use down strokes on the beat keeping the notes short. In the verse, when the rhythm changes, strum down and up on each beat. Watch out for the rests at bar 12 and 16!

The Everly Brothers - The Harmony Brothers?

4 BAR INTRO

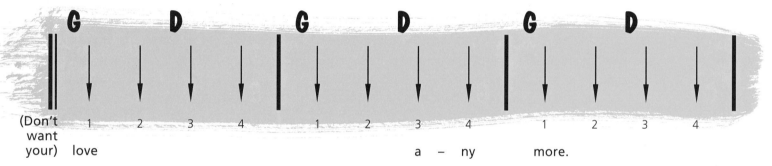

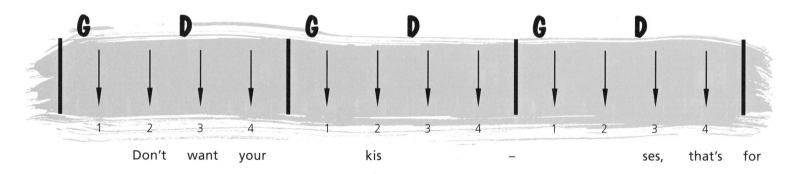

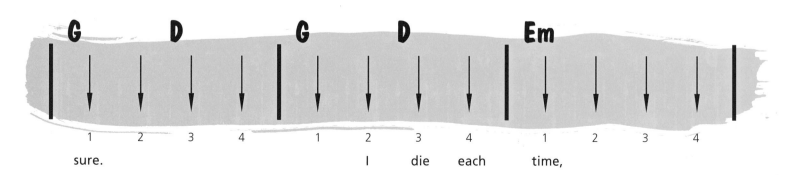

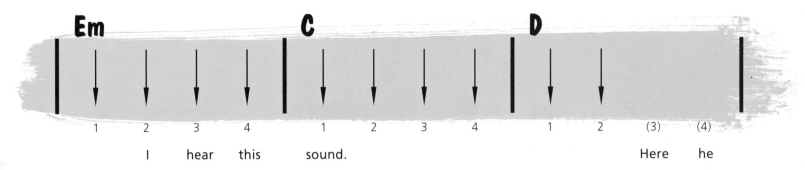

Em   C   D

1   2   3   4   1   2   3   4   1   2   (3)   (4)

I   hear   this   sound.   Here   he

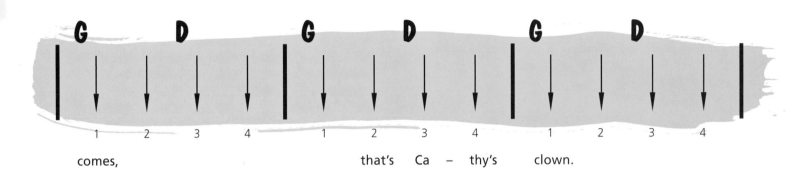

G   D   G   D   G   D

1   2   3   4   1   2   3   4   1   2   3   4

comes,   that's Ca – thy's   clown.

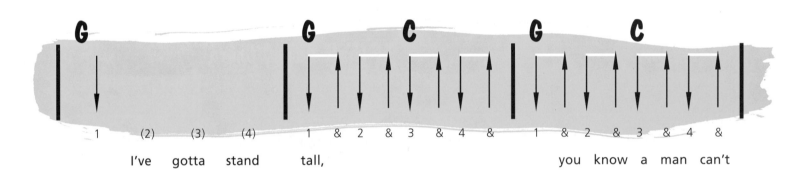

G   G   C   G   C

1   (2)   (3)   (4)   1 & 2 & 3 & 4 &   1 & 2 & 3 & 4 &

I've   gotta   stand   tall,   you know a man can't

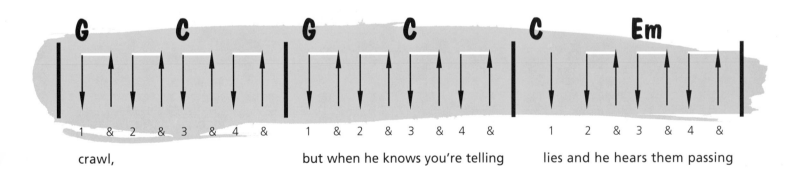

G   C   G   C   C   Em

1 & 2 & 3 & 4 &   1 & 2 & 3 & 4 &   1   2 & 3 & 4 &

crawl,   but when he knows you're telling   lies and he hears them passing

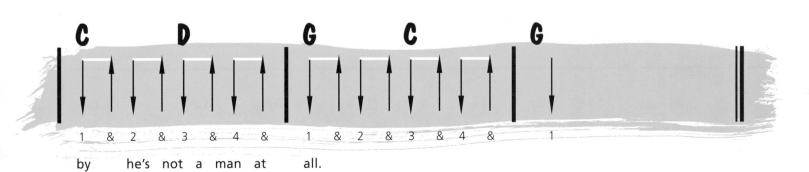

C   D   G   C   G

1 & 2 & 3 & 4 &   1 & 2 & 3 & 4 &   1

by   he's not a man at   all.

Jarvis Cocker — getting back to nature. Word is, his 'forest' gigs are selling out like wildfire…

COMMON PEOPLE
Words by Jarvis Cocker, Music by Pulp

One of the more unusual British acts to hit the charts in the 1990s was Pulp. To play their 1995 single 'Common People' we need the chords C and G, which you already know, plus one more: F major.

How easy or hard you find barre chords depends on several things. First, if the strings on your guitar are too high off the fretboard they will be harder to hold down. Second, you need to keep the first finger quite straight. You may find it easier if you drop the thumb of your fretting hand a little lower behind the neck. **A barre** is not entirely brute strength, there's also a positioning element, so re-position your first finger if you find the strings are lining up with the grooves behind the finger-joints. You should also try to apply pressure with the first finger slightly rolled toward the nut, so that the bonier edge of the finger makes a bit more contact.

Don't worry if the full **F** seems hard at first. Try the second chord box instead, an abbreviated version with a half barre across the top two strings.

F barre Chord

F (half barre) Chord

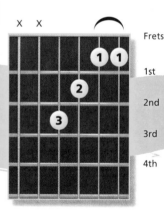

The chords you have learned so far - **C G D A E B7** and **Em** - all have open strings. With **F** major all the strings you strum are fretted with your fingers. One result of this is that you can move the shape up and down the neck to make different major chords. For instance, if you moved your hand to the 2nd fret with this shape you would have the chord of **F♯/G♭** major.

Most of the strumming in '**Common People**' is in 8ths, but to add more interest it can sometimes be a good idea to leave gaps. There are many bars in '**Common People**' where you strum down on the 1st beat but not up on the offbeat.

4 BAR INTRO

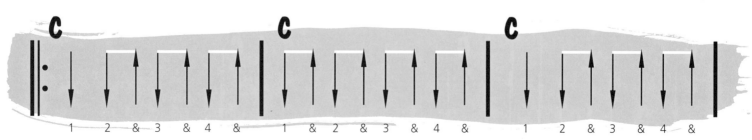

1. She came from Greece, she had a   thirst   for know – ledge,   she studied sculpture at St.
   2. She told me that her   Dad   was loa – ded,   I said in that case I'll have rum and

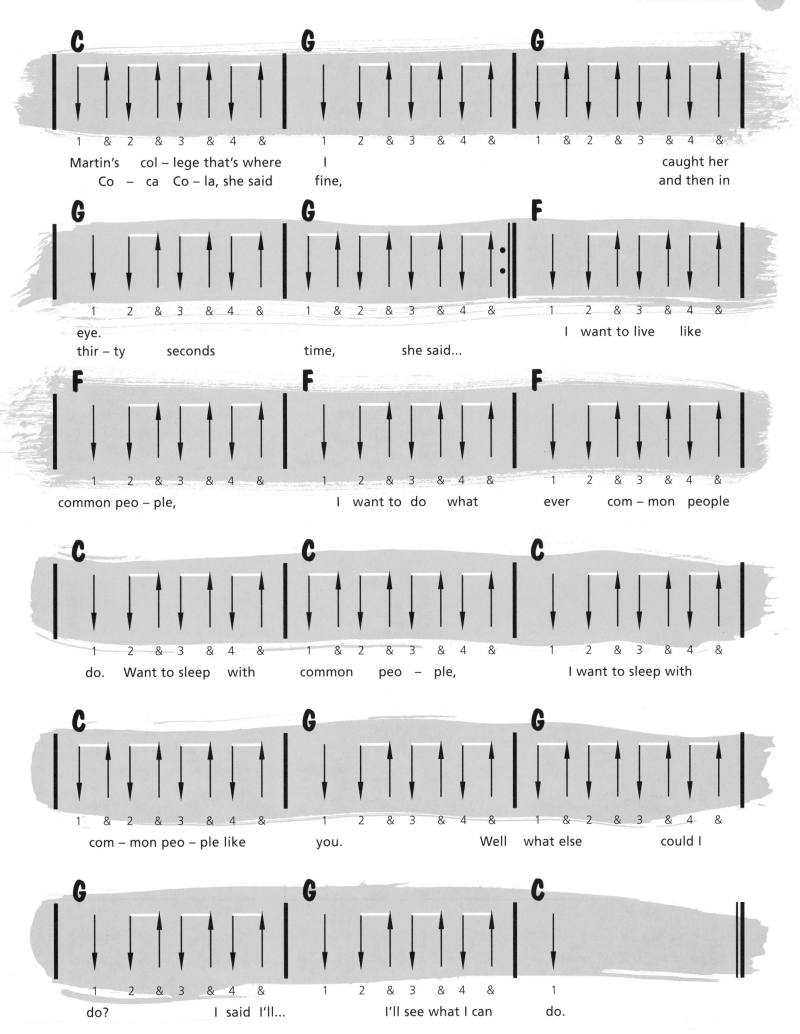

ALL ALONG THE WATCHTOWER
Words & Music by Bob Dylan

Although originally recorded by Bob Dylan on *John Wesley Harding* (1968) and covered by U2 on *Rattle and Hum* (1988), 'All Along The Watchtower' is most closely associated with legendary 60s guitarist Jimi Hendrix.

A minor Chord

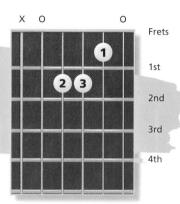

They say other people have more success with Dylan's songs than he did... well it's certainly true in this case!

Although Jimi's recording on *Electric Ladyland* is a staggering display of guitar skills, the basics of the song are very simple. '**All Along The Watchtower**' gives you another opportunity to try **F**, and you need one new chord: **A minor**.

Like **E minor**, **A minor** has a sad, meloncholy sound. It doesn't seem as deep in tone because the 6th string is not played; the root is the open **A** string. One way of remembering the shape is to think of an **E** chord that has been moved down one string. Can you see the resemblance? If you play a song with a change from **Am** to **E** you'll see that it's an easy change because the fingers don't change their shape, only across the strings.

The intro uses the same strum pattern as in '**I Wanna Be Adored**', where there is no strum on the third beat. Notice also that in all the even numbered bars the change from **F** to **G** occurs on the 3rd offbeat.

If you find the **F** chord hard, try using the half-barre shape instead (see page 26).

The CD version sounds in **C minor**, the same key as Hendrix's version, so to play along put a capo at the 3rd fret.

CAPO 3RD FRET
2 BAR CLICK INTRO

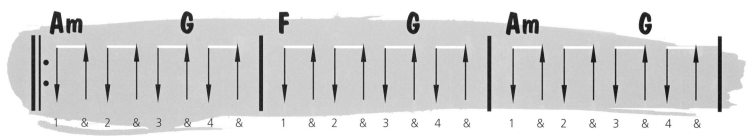

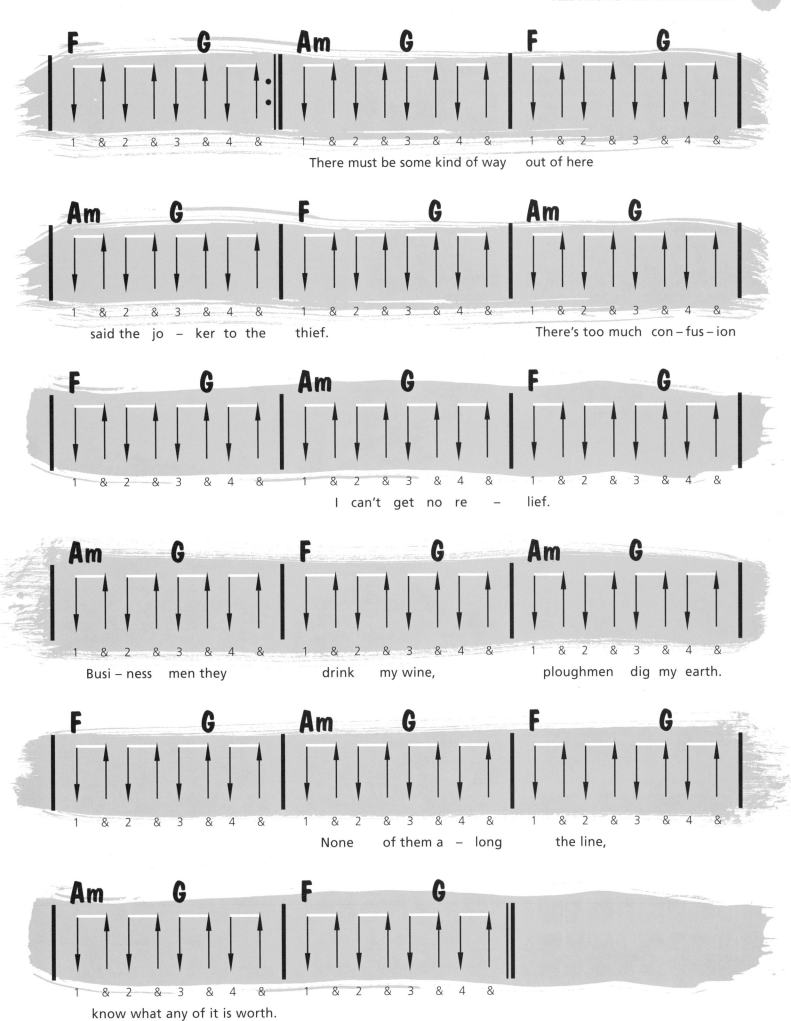

NO WOMAN, NO CRY
Words & Music by Vincent Ford

Bob Marley was reggae's first superstar. He and his band The Wailers achieved this status with a series of hit records that included a live album from a concert at the Lyceum in London in 1975. The atmosphere of that gig is captured on 'No Woman, No Cry'.

This song uses four chords - **C**, **Am**, **F** and **G** - which you have played before. However, the **G** chord is found in a slightly different form. If you found the **F barre** chord hard then **G/B** will be a relief because you only need to use one finger!

G/B Chord

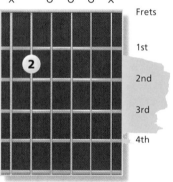

x   o   o   o   X   Frets

1st

2nd

3rd

4th

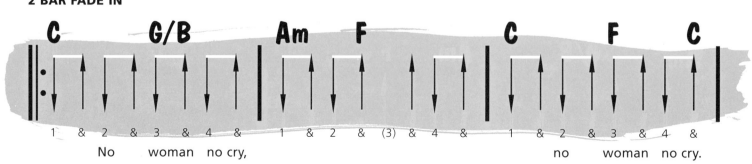

"Me really love 'No Woman, No Cry' because it mean so much to me. Me get so much feeling from it." Bob Marley

This type of chord is known as an 'inversion'. All this means is that the root note (the note after which a chord is named) is not the lowest. One of the other two notes that make a simple major or minor chord is at the bottom. In **G/B B** is the lowest note.

Inversions often occur in chord sequences when the songwriter wants an ascending or descending bass line. **G/B** is popular on the guitar because it is easy to play, and almost always found, as here, between **C** and **Am**.

The strumming is mostly slow 8ths, but look at bar 2. Notice there is no down strum on the 3rd beat. Instead, the **F** is played on the offbeat of the previous 2nd beat. This type of change, coming half a beat before you expect it, is known as an 'anticipation'. Anticipated changes are very important in many forms of popular music. They help to create more of a 'groove'. Listen for the way the **F** chord 'hangs' across the pause in the strumming. If you find the **F** chord hard, use the half-barre version.

2 BAR FADE IN

| C | G/B | Am | F | C | F | C |

1 & 2 & 3 & 4 &   1 & 2 & (3) & 4 &   1 & 2 & 3 & 4 &

No   woman no cry,   no   woman no cry.

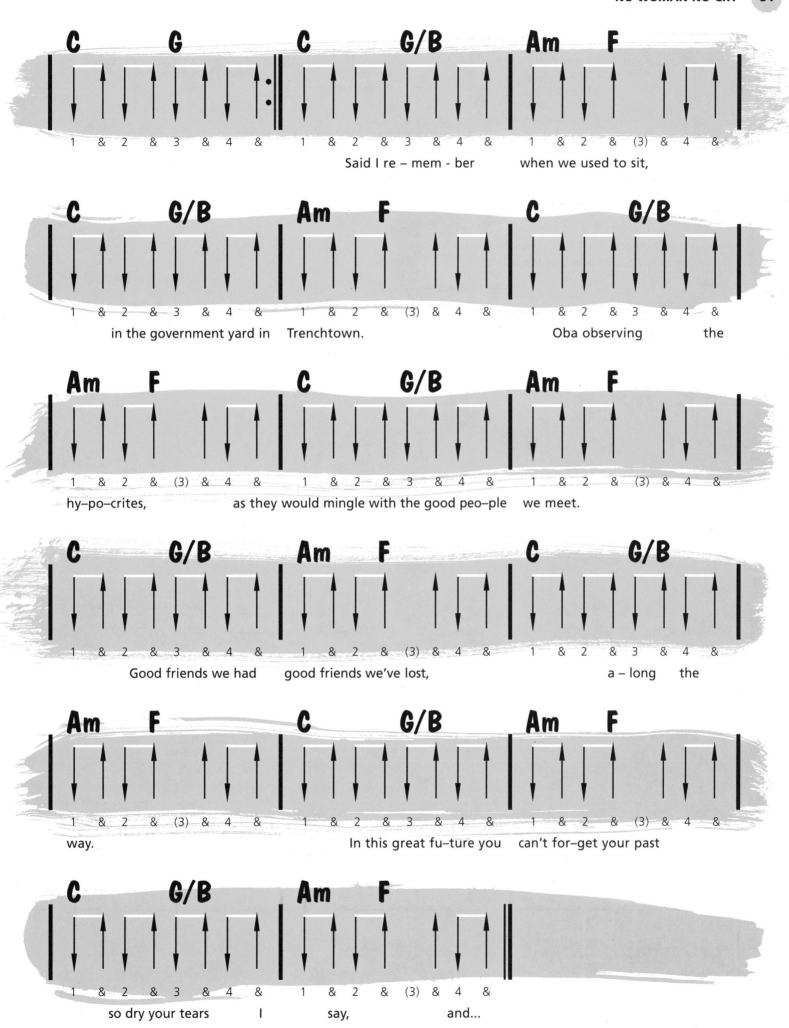

You can hear the original version of this song on Roxy Music's 1979 album Manifesto.

To play this elegant Roxy Music hit from 1979 you need a new minor chord: B minor. This shape is actually derived from Am.

TRACK
24+25
CD1

DANCE AWAY
Words & Music by Bryan Ferry

B minor Chord

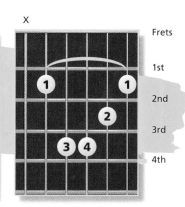

There are no open strings in **Bm**, and it is one of the most important moveable minor shapes. Move it up one fret and it becomes **C minor**, down a fret it becomes **B♭ minor**.

Remember to keep your thumb low down behind the neck for a barre shape such as this. If you wish, you can lay your 2nd finger on top of the 1st to exert a bit more pressure. Play each string individually to make sure that all are sounding.

'Dance Away' uses one strum pattern. Strum down on the 1st beat, wait for the 2nd and then continue with 8ths. To play along with the CD or the original put a capo at the 3rd fret.

CAPO 3RD FRET
8 BAR INTRO

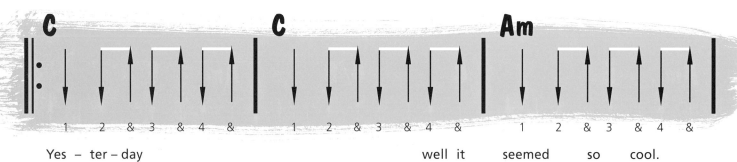

Yes – ter – day   well it   seemed   so   cool.
fun – ny how   I   could   ne – ver   cry.

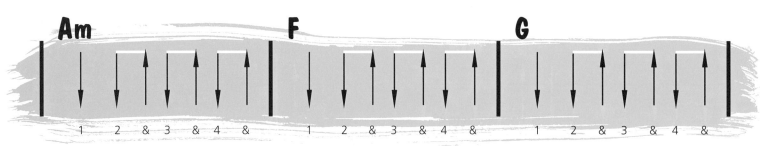

When I   walked you home,   kissed good–night,
Un – til   tonight,   and   you   pass by,

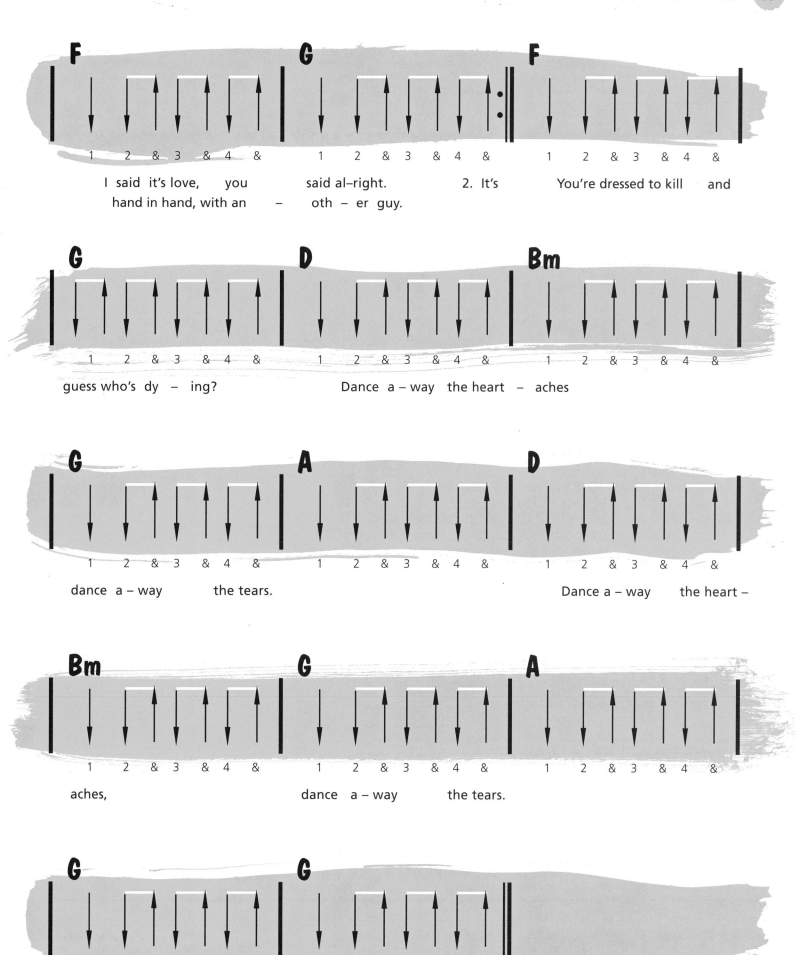

I said it's love,   you   said al–right.   2. It's   You're dressed to kill   and

hand in hand, with an   –   oth – er guy.

guess who's dy – ing?   Dance a – way the heart – aches

dance a – way   the tears.   Dance a – way   the heart –

aches,   dance a – way   the tears.

Dance a – way.

THAT'S ENTERTAINMENT
Words & Music by Paul Weller

Am7 Chord

x o o o

Frets
1st
2nd
3rd
4th

Em7 Chord

o   o   o

Frets
1st
2nd
3rd
4th

In 1980, Paul Weller wrote this hit song, signifying a shift away from The Jam's trademark aggressive power chords.

'**That's Entertainment**' manages to combine a haunting lyric with a driving acoustic rhythm and uses only four chords. You already know G and Fmaj7. The two new chords are variations on Am and Em, and they're both very easy.

Em7 is similarly easy – you can play **Em** and then add your fourth finger. Notice how adding the 7th 'softens' the sound of the minor chord – now it doesn't sound as sad.

Am7 is simply **Am** with the third finger lifted off. Let the open strings ring out, but beware not to let the bottom E string sound. Either strum from the 5th string downwards, or try muting the string with your fretting hand thumb.

You'll see that on the last beat of some of the bars there's that quick 16th up-and-down figure that you first tried out with '**Stand By Me**'. Listen for the effect of the even-numbered bars where **Em7** turns into Em as you lift your little finger off the 2nd string.

Like the original recording, the CD track for '**That's Entertainment**' features a capo at the 3rd fret.

The intro is 8 bars long - again, practise counting to find out where you should start playing.

Paul Weller – a Modern Classic.

CAPO 3RD FRET
8 BAR INTRO

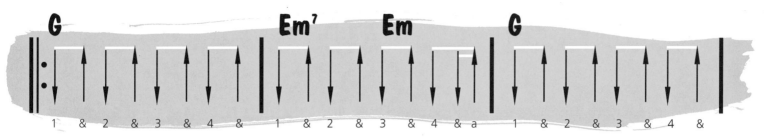

1. A pol–ice car   and a   screaming   si – ren,   pneu–ma–tic drill   and
2. A smash of glass and a   rumble   of   boots,   an electric train   and a

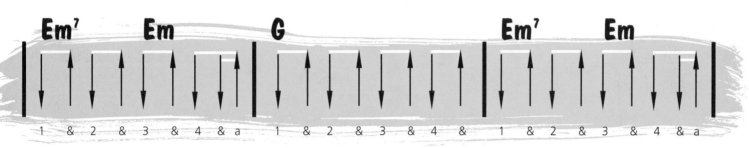

ripped up   con – crete.   A ba – by wailing a stray   dog how – ling,
ripped up   phone   booth.   Paint-splattered walls and the   cry of a tom - cat,

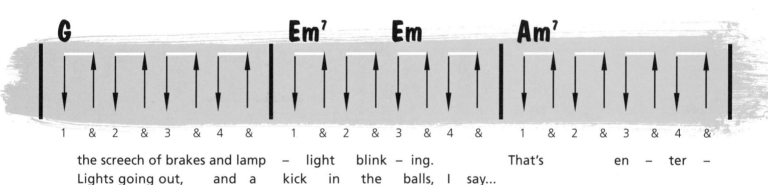

the screech of brakes and lamp   – light   blink – ing.   That's   en – ter –
Lights going out,   and a   kick in   the   balls, I say...

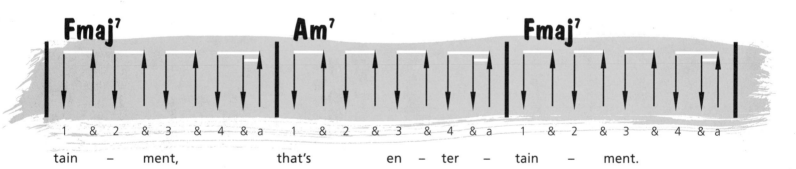

tain –   ment,   that's   en – ter – tain – ment.

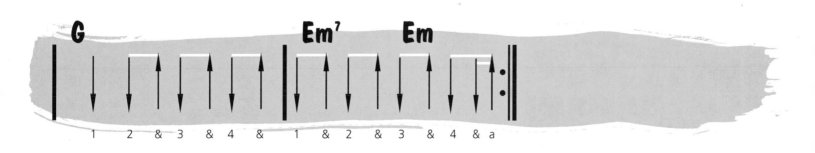

SIT DOWN

Words & Music by Tim Booth, Larry Gott, Gavan Whelan & Jim Glennie

B major Chord

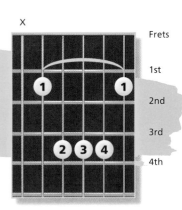

James' 1991 hit introduces the chord of B major. The B major chord like the Bm chord is derived from the shape for A.

If you find this difficult you can simplify it by taking the barre off. Then the 1st finger just holds down the 2nd fret of the top string. If you play B this way you must be careful not to strum either the 5th or 6th strings. Along with the full **F**, **B** is the most important movable major barre shape.

Like several of the earlier songs this has a shuffle feel in which each pair of 8ths is no longer even, but the first is longer than the second. If you wish you can substitute **B7** for the **B** chord while you get used to the changes. Since this song features a chord change from **A** to **B** you could experiment holding the **A** chord down with your 2nd, 3rd and 4th fingers. These all become guide fingers when you change to **B**.

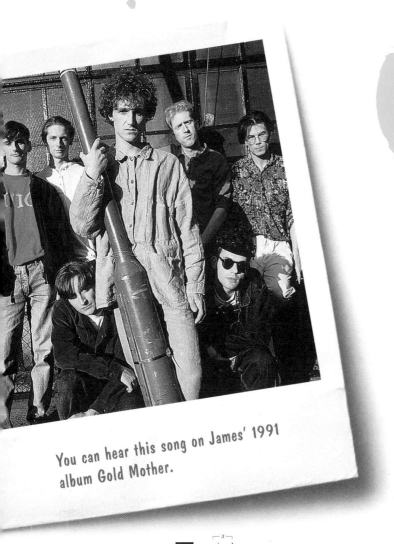

You can hear this song on James' 1991 album Gold Mother.

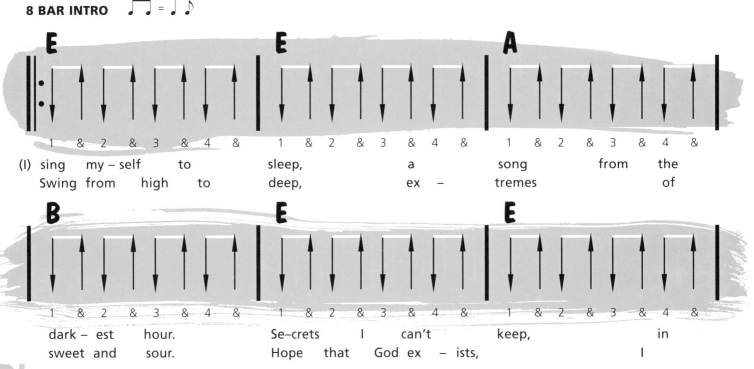

8 BAR INTRO

(I) sing my–self to sleep, a song from the
Swing from high to deep, ex – tremes of

dark – est hour. Se–crets I can't keep, in
sweet and sour. Hope that God ex – ists, I

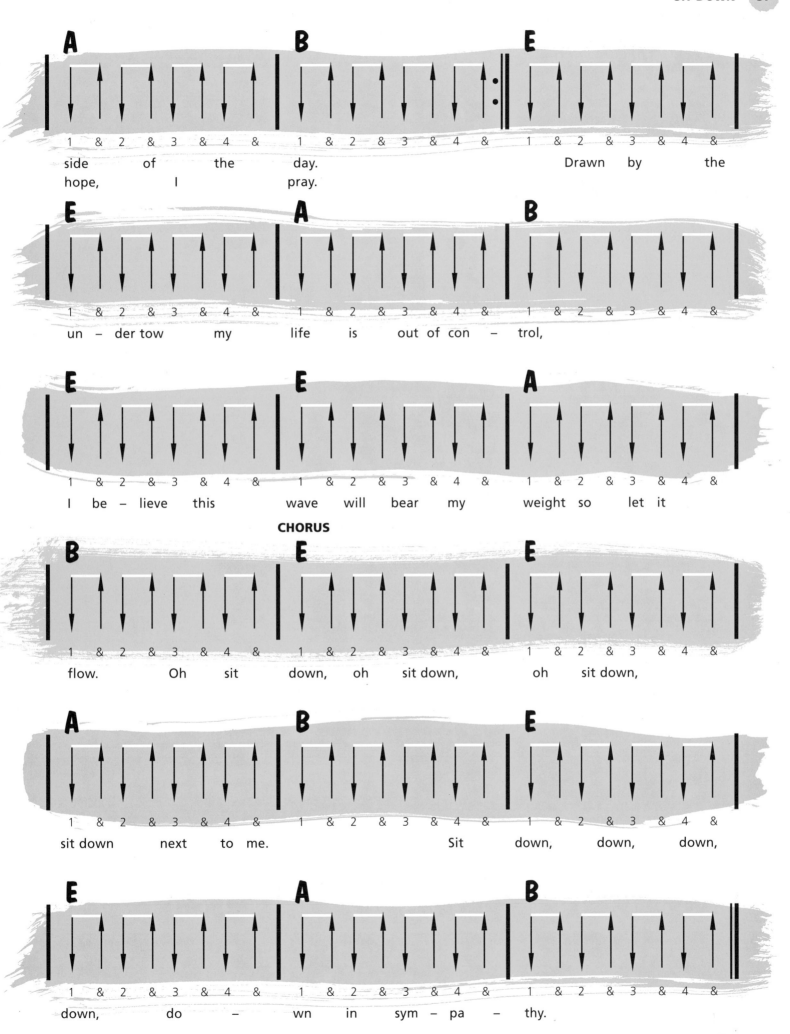

SO FAR AWAY
Words & Music by Mark Knopfler

C#m Chord

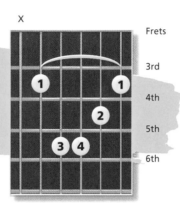

X

Frets

3rd

4th

5th

6th

This track from Dire Straits' best-selling album *Brothers In Arms* features an easy, relaxed strum, and one new chord: **C#m**

The **C#** **minor** chord is the **B minor** chord moved up two frets. If you find this difficult you can simplify it by taking the barre off. Then the 1st finger just holds down the 4th fret of the top string. If you play **C#m** this way you must be careful not to strum either the 5th or 6th strings.

To emulate the chugging 8th note rhythm of the original, try damping the chords. You do this by resting the side of your strumming hand on the strings very close to the tailpiece (where the strings are fixed to the body). Don't make too much contact or the strings won't make enough sound. If you get it right it just takes the ring out of them. Then you can concentrate on hitting the lower notes of each chord.

When you change from **E** to **C#m** in the chorus watch your 3rd finger on the fretting hand. It's a guide finger. Notice that it does not go to a *different* string; it goes up the 4th string.

Mark Knopfler's trademark bottleneck licks have always been instantly recognisable — and this track is no exception.

4 BAR FADE IN

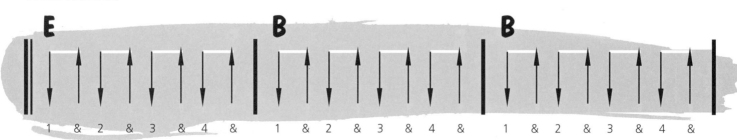

E				B				B			

1 & 2 & 3 & 4 &   1 & 2 & 3 & 4 &   1 & 2 & 3 & 4 &

Here I am a – gain in this   mean old   town,   and you're so far a – way

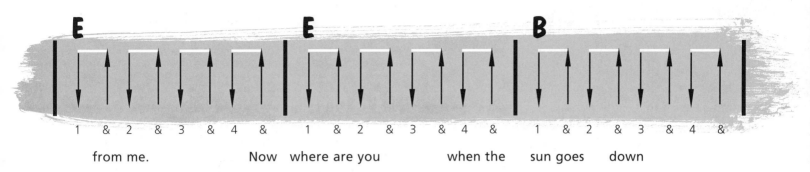

1 & 2 & 3 & 4 &   1 & 2 & 3 & 4 &   1 & 2 & 3 & 4 &

from me.　　Now where are you　when the　sun goes　down

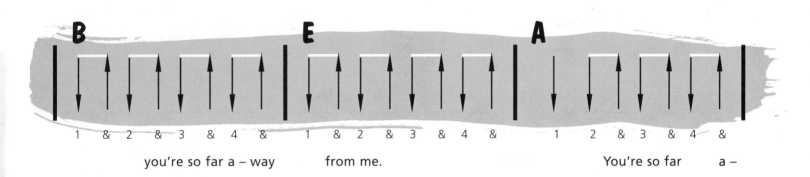

1 & 2 & 3 & 4 &   1 & 2 & 3 & 4 &   1　2 & 3 & 4 &

you're so far a – way　from me.　　You're so far　a –

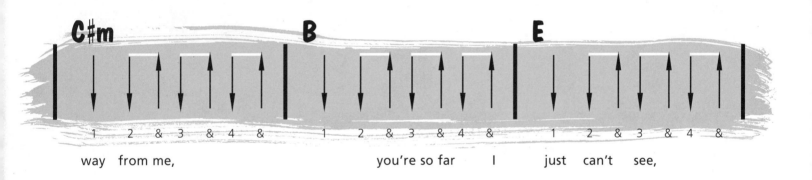

1　2 & 3 & 4 &   1　2 & 3 & 4 &   1　2 & 3 & 4 &

way from me,　　you're so far　I　just can't see,

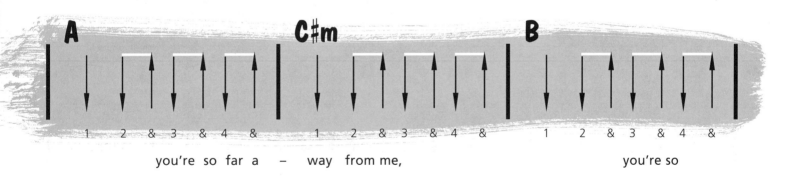

1　2 & 3 & 4 &   1　2 & 3 & 4 &   1　2 & 3 & 4 &

you're so far a　–　way from me,　　you're so

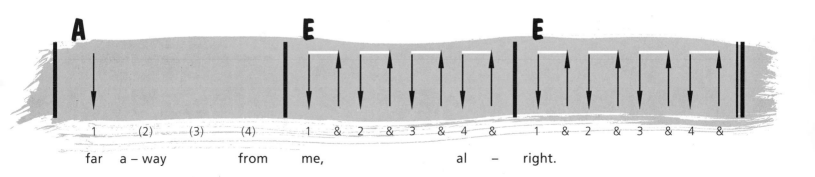

1　(2)　(3)　(4)   1 & 2 & 3 & 4 &   1 & 2 & 3 & 4 &

far a – way　　from me,　　al　–　right.

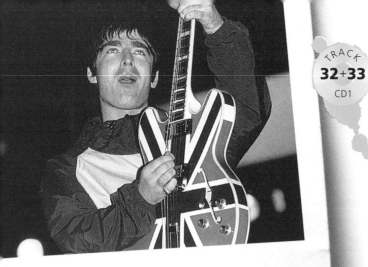

TRACK
32+33
CD1

HALF THE WORLD AWAY
Words & Music by Noel Gallagher

This song was originally the B-side to the single
'Whatever', but has since become better known as
the theme tune to the TV series The Royle Family.

Fm Chord

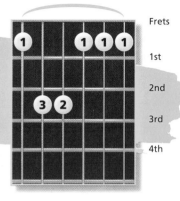

G7 Chord

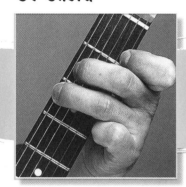
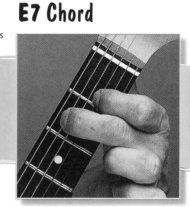

E7 Chord

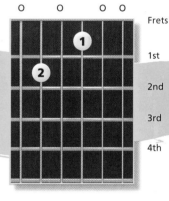

There are three new chords in this song:
E7, G7 and Fm. The Fm chord is created by
taking the Em you learned in 'I Wanna Be
Adored' and turning it into a barre chord.

The relaxed, lazy strum of this song owes much to the
use of the tied 2nd offbeat, which you have played before.
Where indicated there are some bars where you play the
root note on its own and then strum the chord. These are
indicated by a number under the arrow (the number is the
string on which the root note can be found).

4 BAR INTRO

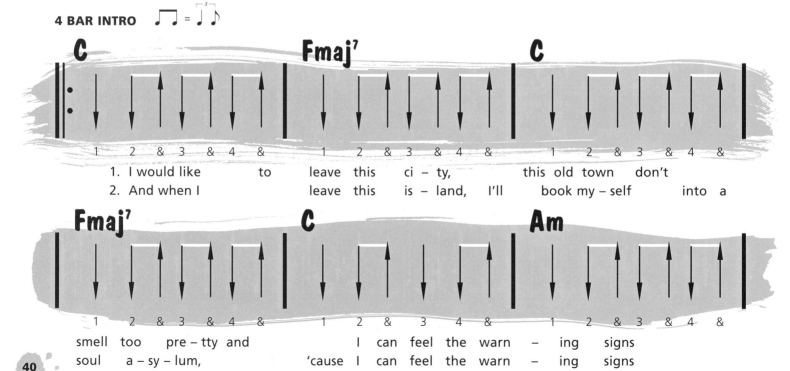

C   Fmaj⁷   C

1. I would like   to   leave this   ci – ty,   this old town   don't
2. And when I   leave this   is – land, I'll   book my – self   into a

Fmaj⁷   C   Am

smell too   pre – tty and   I can feel the warn – ing signs
soul   a – sy – lum,   'cause I can feel the warn – ing signs

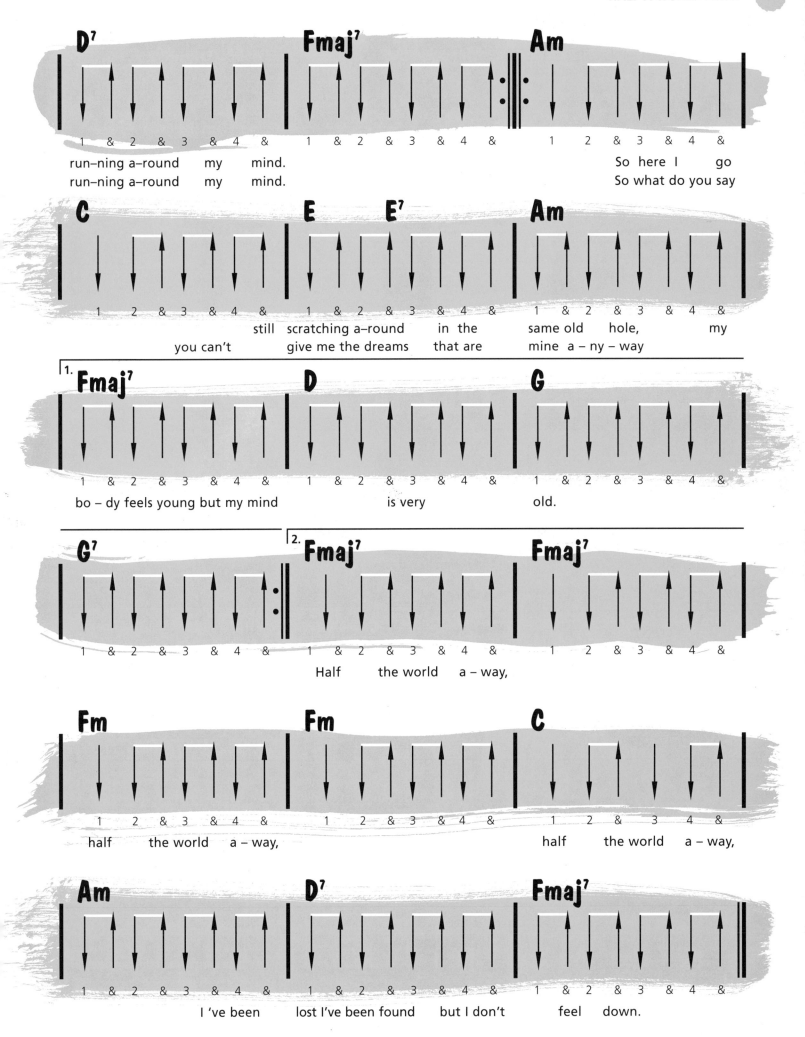

AMERICAN PIE
Words & Music by Don McLean

A7 Chord

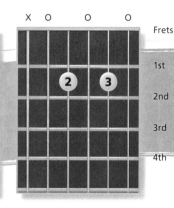

D/F♯ Chord

D7 Chord

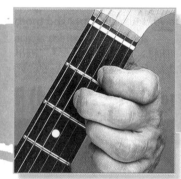

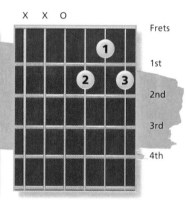

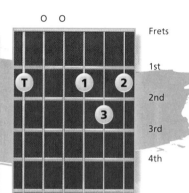

Madonna tried to make this song hip in 2000 but let's face it, it's still just a 'good ole boys' country tune.

This song by singer-songwriter Don McLean was inspired by the death of Buddy Holly in a plane crash in February 1959. Originally a hit in 1972, it recently charted again when it was covered by Madonna.

To play this song you will need three new chords: **D7**, **D/F♯** and **A7**.

D/F♯ is another inverted chord. Along with **G/B** (which you have already met) it is the most common inversion on the guitar. It is often found, as here, between **G** and **Em**.

The strumming is mostly straight 8ths, with the occasional bar in which the second offbeat is tied across beat 3. There are also bars where the chord rings for the entire bar.

So far with *The Complete Rock & Pop Guitar Player* you have learned 17 songs, 20 chords, a number of strumming patterns, and you're starting to get to grips with barre chords. There are more great songs to play in Parts 2 and 3, and the chance to play some easy riffs and other single note phrases.

See you in Part 2!

2 BAR INTRO

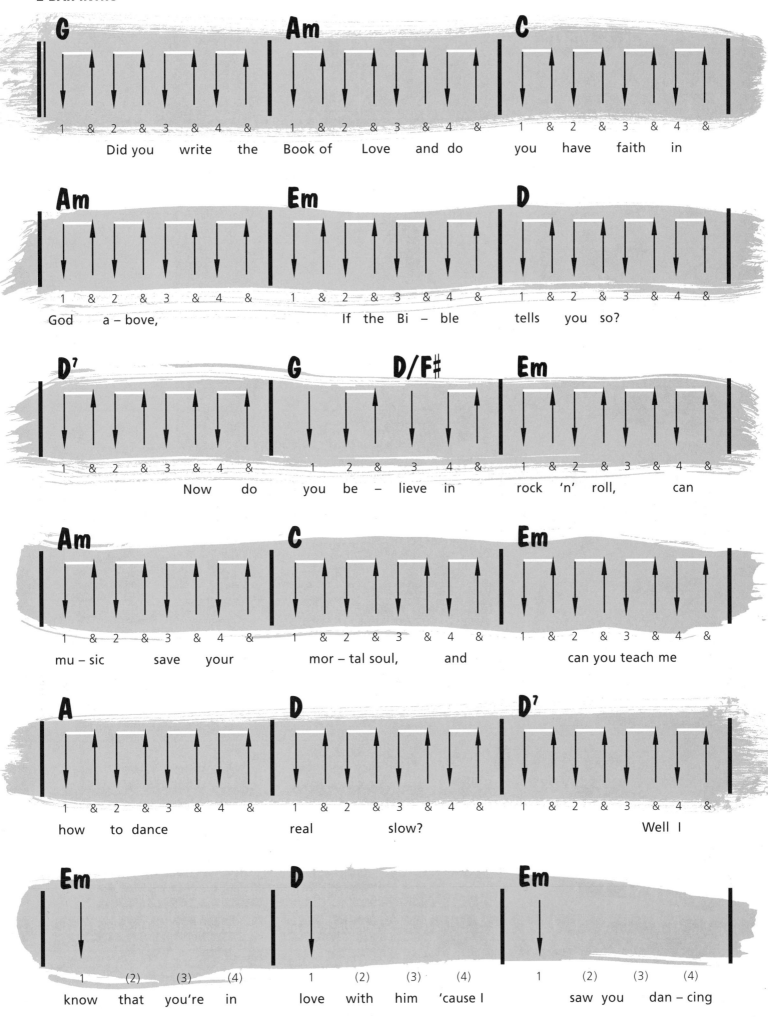

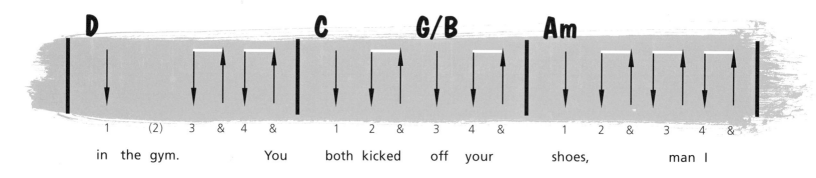

D   **C**   **G/B**   **Am**

1   (2)   3 & 4 &   1   2 & 3 & 4 &   1   2 & 3 & 4 &

in the gym.   You   both kicked off your   shoes,   man I

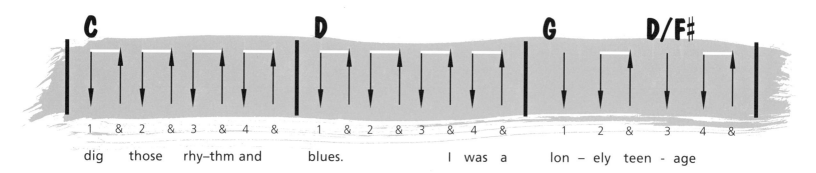

C   **D**   **G**   **D/F#**

1 & 2 & 3 & 4 &   1 & 2 & 3 & 4 &   1   2 & 3   4 &

dig those rhy–thm and   blues.   I was a   lon – ely teen - age

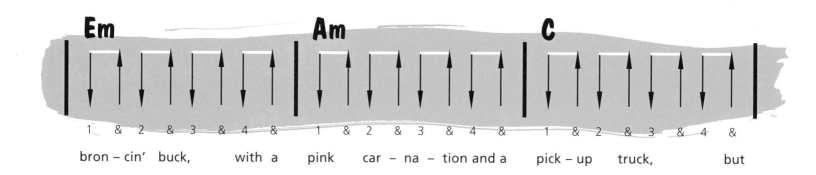

Em   **Am**   **C**

1 & 2 & 3 & 4 &   1 & 2 & 3 & 4 &   1 & 2 & 3 & 4 &

bron – cin' buck,   with a   pink car – na – tion and a   pick – up truck,   but

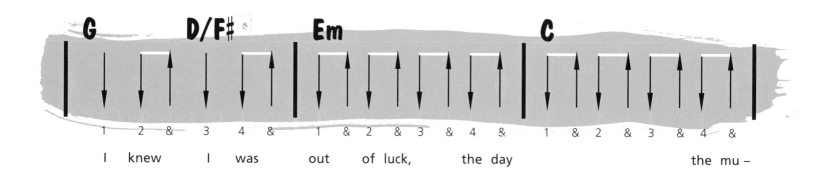

G   **D/F#**   **Em**   **C**

1   2 & 3   4 &   1 & 2 & 3 & 4 &   1 & 2 & 3 & 4 &

I knew   I was   out   of luck,   the day   the mu –

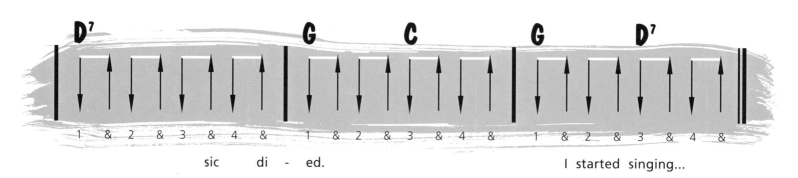

D⁷   **G**   **C**   **G**   **D⁷**

1 & 2 & 3 & 4 &   1 & 2 & 3 & 4 &   1 & 2 & 3 & 4 &

       sic   di – ed.   I started singing...

ADDITIONAL LYRICS

PAPERBACK WRITER

Paperback writer, Paperback writer...

Verse 1
Dear Sir or Madam,
will you read my book,
It took me years to write,
will you take a look?
It's based on a novel
by a man named Lear,
And I need a job,
So I want to be a paperback writer,
Paperback writer.

Verse 2
It's a dirty story of a dirty man,
And his clinging wife
doesn't understand.
His son is working for the Daily Mail,
It's a steady job,
But he wants to be a paperback writer,
Paperback writer.

Paperback writer, Paperback writer...

Verse 3
It's a thousand pages, give or take a few,
I'll be writing more in a week or two.
I can make it longer if you like the style,
I can change it round,
And I want to be a paperback writer,
Paperback writer.

Verse 4
If you really like it
you can have the rights,
It could make a million for you
overnight,
If you must return it,
you can send it here,
But I need a break
And I want to be a paperback writer,
Paperback writer.

Paperback writer, Paperback writer...

BRIMFUL OF ASHA

Verse 1
There's dancing behind movie scenes,
Behind the movie scenes Sadi Rani,
She's the one that keeps the dream alive
From the morning past the evening
To the end of the light.

Chorus
Brimful of Asha on the forty-five,
Well it's a brimful of Asha on the
forty-five.

Verse 2
And singing, illuminate the main streets
And the cinema aisles,
We don't care about no government
warnings
'Bout their promotion of the simple life
And the dams they're building.

Chorus

Bridge
Everybody needs a bosom for a pillow,
Everybody needs a bosom.
Mine's on the forty-five.

Verse 3
Mohamid Rufi. (Forty-five).
Lata Mangeskar. (Forty-five).
Solid state radio. (Forty-five).
Ferguson mono (Forty-five).
Bon Publeek (Forty-five).
Jacques Dutronc and the Bolan Boogie,
The Heavy Hitters and the chi-chi music,
All India radio.
Two-in-ones.
Argo records.
Trojan records.

Chorus

Bridge

Coda
Seventy-thousand piece orchestra set.
Everybody needs a bosom for a pillow,
Mine's on the r.p.m.

Brimful of Asha on the forty-five,
Well it's a brimful of Asha on the
forty-five.

Everybody needs a bosom for a pillow,
Everybody needs a bosom.
Mine's on the forty-five.

HELLO, I LOVE YOU

Chorus

Hello, I love you
Won't you tell me your name?
Hello, I love you,
Let me jump in your game.

Chorus

Verse 1
She's walking down the street
Blind to every eye she meets.
Do you think you'll be the guy
To make the queen of the angels sigh?

Chorus

Chorus

Verse 2
She holds her head so high
Like a statue in the sky.
Her arms are wicked and her legs are
long,
When she moves, my brain screams out
this song.

Verse 3
Sidewalk crouches at her feet
Like a dog that begs for something
sweet.
Do you hope to make her see, you fool?
Do you hope to pluck this dusky jewel?

Hello, hello, hello, hello.

ROCK AROUND THE CLOCK

Intro
One, two, three o'clock,
four o'clock rock,
Five, six, seven o'clock,
eight o'clock rock,
Nine, ten, eleven o'clock,
twelve o'clock rock,
We're gonna rock around
the clock tonight!

Verse 1
Put your glad rags on and join me, Hon,
We'll have some fun when the clock
strikes one,
We're gonna rock around the
clock tonight,
We're gonna rock, rock, rock 'til
broad daylight,
We're gonna rock, gonna rock,
around the clock tonight.

Verse 2
When the clock strikes two,
and three and four,
If the band shows down
we'll ask for more,
We're gonna rock around the
clock tonight,
We're gonna rock, rock, rock 'til
broad daylight,
We're gonna rock, gonna rock,
around the clock tonight.

Verse 3
When the chimes ring five, six and
seven,
We'll be ridin' seventh heaven,
We're gonna rock around the clock
tonight,
We're gonna rock, rock, rock 'til
broad daylight,
We're gonna rock, gonna rock,
around the clock tonight.

Verse 4
When it's eight, nine, ten, eleven too,
I'll be goin' strong and so will you,
We're gonna rock around the
clock tonight,
We're gonna rock, rock, rock 'til
broad daylight,
We're gonna rock, gonna rock,
around the clock tonight.

Verse 5
When the clock strikes twelve,
we'll cool off, then
Start-a-rockin' round the
clock again,
We're gonna rock around the clock
tonight,
We're gonna rock, rock, rock 'til
broad daylight,
We're gonna rock, gonna rock,
around the clock tonight.

THAT'LL BE THE DAY

Chorus
Well, that'll be the day, when you say
goodbye
Yes that'll be the day, when you make
me cry
You say you're gonna leave, you know
it's a lie
'Cause that'll be the day when I die.

Verse 1
Well, you give me all your lovin' and
your turtle dovin'
All your hugs and kisses and your
money too
Well you know you love me baby
Until you tell me, maybe
That some day, well, I'll be through!

Chorus

Verse 2
When Cupid shot his dart, he shot it at
your heart
So if we ever part and I leave you
You say you told me and you told me
boldly
That some day, well, I'll be through.

Chorus

I WANNA BE ADORED

Verse 1
I don't need to sell my soul
He's already in me,
I don't need to sell my soul
He's already in me.

Chorus
I wanna be adored.
I wanna be adored.

Verse 2
I don't need to sell my soul
He's already in me,
I don't need to sell my soul
He's already in me.

Chorus

Bridge
Adored.
I wanna be adored.
You adore me, you adore me,
you adore me.
I wanna, I wanna, I wanna be adored.
I wanna, I wanna, I wanna be adored.
I wanna, I wanna, I wanna be adored.
I wanna, I wanna, I gotta be adored.

I wanna be adored.

STAND BY ME

Verse 1
When the night has come
And the land is dark
And the moon is the only light we'll see
No I won't be afraid
No I won't be afraid
Just as long as you stand, stand by me.

Chorus
So darling, darling, stand by me
Oh, stand by me.
Oh, stand, stand by me, stand by me.

Verse 2
If the sky that we look upon
Should tumble and fall
Or the mountain should crumble into
the sea
I won't cry, I won't cry
No I won't shed a tear
Just as long as you stand, stand by me.

Chorus

CATHY'S CLOWN

Chorus
Don't want your love anymore,
Don't want your kisses back for sure.
I die each time I hear this sound:
Here he comes - that's Cathy's clown.

Verse 1
I've gotta stand tall,
You know a man can't crawl
But when he knows you're telling lies
And he hears them passing by
Then he's not a man at all.

Chorus

Verse 2
When you see me shed a tear
And you know that it's sincere,
But wouldn't you think it's kinda sad
That you're treating me so bad
Or do you even care?

Chorus

COMMON PEOPLE

Verse 1
She came from Greece, she had a thirst
for knowledge,
She studied sculpture at St.Martin's
college,
That's where I caught her eye.
She told me that her Dad was loaded,
I said, "In that case I'll have rum and
Coca-Cola,"
She said, "Fine."
And then in thirty seconds time she said,

Chorus
"I want to live like common people,
I want to do whatever common people
do,
Want to sleep with common people,
I want to sleep with common people
Like you."
Well, what else could I do?
I said, "I'll ... I'll see what I can do."

Verse 2
I took her to a supermarket,
I don't know why but I had to start it
somewhere, so it started there.

I said, "Pretend you've got no money,"
She just laughed and said, "Oh, you're
so funny," I said, "Yeah?"
(Well I can't see anyone else smiling
in here),
Are you sure?

Chorus
"You want to live like common people,
You want to see whatever common
people see,
You want to sleep with common people,
You want to sleep with common people
like me."

Verse 3
Rent a flat above a shop, cut your hair
and get a job,
Smoke some fags and play some pool,
pretend you never went to school,
But still you'll never get it right 'cause
when you're laid in bed at night
Watching 'roaches climb the wall,
If you called your Dad he could stop it
all, yeah.

Chorus
You'll never live like common people,
You'll never do whatever common
people do;
You'll never fail like common people,
You'll never watch your life slide out of
view
And then dance and drink and screw
Because there's nothing else to do.

Chorus
Sing along with the common people,
Sing along and it might just get you
through.
Laugh along with the common people,
Laugh along even though they're
laughing at you
And the stupid things that you do,
Because you think that poor is cool.

Bridge
Like a dog lying in the corner,
They will bite you and never warn you,
Look out, they'll tear your insides out,
'Cause everybody hates a tourist,
Especially one who thinks it's all such a
laugh,
And the chip stains and grease will come
out in the bath.
You will never understand how it feels
to live your life
With no meaning or control and
nowhere left to go.
You are amazed that they exist
And they burn so bright whilst you can
only wonder why.

Verse 4
Rent a flat above a shop, cut your hair
and get a job,
Smoke some fags and play some pool,
pretend you never went to school,
But still you'll never get it right 'cause
when you're laid in bed at night
Watching 'roaches climb the wall,
If you called your Dad he could stop it
all, yeah.

Chorus
You'll never live like common people,
You'll never do whatever common
people do,
You'll never fail like common people,
You'll never watch your life slide out of
view
And then dance and drink and screw
Because there's nothing else to do.

Want to live with common people
like you.

ALL ALONG THE WATCHTOWER

Verse 1
"There must be some way out of here,"
Said the joker to the thief,
"There's too much confusion,
I can't get no relief.
Business men, they drink my wine,
Ploughmen dig my earth,
None of them along the line
Know what any of it is worth."

Verse 2
"No reason to get excited,"
The thief he kindly spoke,
"There are many here among us
Who feel that life is but a joke.
But you and I we've been through that,
And this is not our fate,
So let us not talk falsely now,
The hour is getting late."

Verse 3
All along the watchtower
Princes kept the view
While other women came and went,
Barefoot servants, too.
Outside in the distance
A wildcat did growl,
Two riders were approaching,
The wind began to howl.

NO WOMAN, NO CRY

Chorus
No woman, no cry, no woman, no cry.
No woman, no cry, no woman, no cry.

Verse 1
Say, say, said I remember
when we used to sit
In the government yard in Trenchtown,
Oba-observing the hypocrites
As they would mingle with the good
people we meet.
Good friends we have had,
oh good friends we've lost
Along the way.
In this bright future you can't forget
your past,
So dry your tears, I say, and...

Chorus

Verse 2
Said, said, said I remember
when we used to sit
In the government yard in Trenchtown,
And then Georgie would make the fire
light
As it was log wood burning through the
night.
Then we would cook corn meal porridge
Of which I'll share with you.
My feet is my only carriage
So I've got to push on through,
But while I'm gone I mean...

Bridge
Everything's gonna be alright,
Everything's gonna be alright.

Chorus
No woman, no cry, no no woman, no
woman, no cry.
Oh little sister, don't shed no tears,
No woman, no cry.

Verse 3
Said, said, said I remember
when we used to sit
In the government yard in Trenchtown,
And then Georgie would make
the fire light
As it was log wood burning through
the night.
Then we would cook corn meal porridge
Of which I'll share with you.
My feet is my only carriage
So I've got to push on through,
But while I'm gone I mean ...

Chorus
No woman, no cry, no woman, no cry.
Oh c'mon little darlin', say don't shed no
tears,
No woman, no cry.

DANCE AWAY

Verse 1
Yesterday, well it seemed so cool
When I walked you home, kissed
goodnight
I said "It's Love", you said "Alright"
It's funny how I could never cry
Until tonight and you pass by
Hand in hand with another guy
You're dressed to kill and guess who's
dying?

Chorus
Dance away the heartaches,
dance away the tears
Dance away the heartaches,
dance away the tears
Dance away

Verse 2
Loneliness is a crowded room
Full of open hearts, turned to stone
All together, all alone.
All at once my whole world had changed
Now I'm in the dark, off the wall
Let the strobe light up them all
I close my eyes and dance till dawn

Chorus

Verse 3
Now I know I must walk the line
Until I find an open door
Off the street on to the floor
There was I many times a fool
I hope and pray but not too much
Out of reach is out of touch
All the way is far enough

Chorus

Outro
Dance away, dance away, dance away
Dance away the heartaches,
dance away the tears
Dance away the heartaches,
dance away the tears
Dance away the heartaches,
dance away the tears
Dance away the heartaches,
dance away the tears.

THAT'S ENTERTAINMENT

Verse 1
A police car and a screaming siren,
Pneumatic drill and ripped up concrete;
A baby wailing, a stray dog howling,
The screech of brakes and lamplight
blinking:
That's entertainment,
that's entertainment.

Verse 2
A smash of glass and the rumble
of boots,
An electric train and a ripped-up phone
booth,
Paint-splattered walls and the cry of
a tom-cat,
Lights going out, and a kick in the balls.
That's entertainment,
that's entertainment.

Verse 3
Days of speed and slow-time Mondays,
Pissing down with rain on a boring
Wednesday;
Watching the news and not eating
your tea,
A freezing cold flat and damp on
the walls.
I say, that's entertainment,
that's entertainment.

Verse 4
Waking up at 6.00 a.m. on a cold warm
morning,
Opening the windows and breathing
in petrol;
An amateur band rehearsing in
a nearby yard,
Watching the telly and thinking 'bout
your holidays
That's entertainment,
that's entertainment.

Verse 5
Waking up from bad dreams and
smoking cigarettes,
Cuddling a warm girl and smelling
stale perfume;
A hot summer's day and sticky black
tarmac,
Feeding ducks in the park and wishing
you were far away.
That's entertainment,
that's entertainment.

Verse 6

Two lovers kissing amongst the scream
of midnight,
Two lovers missing the tranquility of
solitude;
Getting a cab and travelling on buses,
Reading the graffiti about slashed seat
affairs.
I said, that's entertainment,
that's entertainment.

SIT DOWN

Verse 1

I sing myself to sleep
A song from the darkest hour,
Secrets I can't keep inside all the day.
Swing from high to deep, extremes of
sweet and sour.
Hope that God exists, I hope, I pray,
Torn by the undertow, my life is out of
control;
I believe this wave will bear my weight
so let it roll.

Chorus

Oh sit down, oh sit down, oh sit down,
Sit down next to me
Sit down, down, down, down
Down in sympathy.

Verse 2

Now I'm relieved to hear that you've
been to some far-out places.
It's hard to carry on when you feel all
alone,
Now I've swung back down again it's
worse than it was before.
If I had not seen such riches I could live
with being poor.

Chorus

Those who feel the breath of sadness
Sit down next to me,
Those who find they're touched by
madness
Sit down next to me,
Those who find themselves ridiculous
Sit down next to me.
In love, in fear, in hate, in tears.,
In love, in fear, in hate, in tears,
In love, in fear, in hate, in tears,
In love, in fear, in hate.

Chorus

SO FAR AWAY

Verse 1

Here I am again in this mean old town
And you're so far away from me,
And where are you when the sun goes
down?
You're so far away from me.

Chorus

So far away from me,
So far I just can't see,
So far away from me,
You're so far away from me.

Verse 2

I'm tired of being in love and being all
alone
When you're so far away from me.
I'm tired of making out on the
telephone
'Cause you're so far away from me.

Chorus

Verse 3

I get so tired when I have to explain
When you're so far away from me.
See you've been in the sun and I've been
in the rain
And you're so far away from me.

Chorus

You're so far away from me

HALF THE WORLD AWAY

Verse 1

I would like to leave this city,
This old town don't smell too pretty,
And I can feel the warning signs
Running around my mind.
And when I leave this island
I'll book myself into a soul asylum
'Cause I can feel the warning signs
Running around my mind.

Prechorus

So here I go,
Still scratching around in the same
old hole,
My body is young but my mind feels
very old.

Chorus

So what do you say?
You can't give me the dreams that are
mine anyway.
Half the world away, half the world
away,
Half the world away:
I've been lost I've been found but
I don't feel down.

Verse 2

And when I leave this planet
You know I'd stay
but I just can't stand it,
And I can feel the warning signs
Running around my mind.
And if I could leave this spirit
I'd find me a hole and I'd live in it
And I can feel the warning signs
Running around my mind.

Prechorus

Here I go I'm still scratching around in
the same old hole,
My body feels young but my mind is
very old.

Chorus

No, I don't feel down.

AMERICAN PIE

Verse 1
A long, long time ago, I can still
remember
How that music used to make me smile,
And I knew if I had my chance
That I could make those people dance
And maybe they'd be happy for a while.
But February made me shiver with every
paper I'd deliver.
Bad news on the doorstep, I couldn't
take one more step.
I can't remember if I cried when I read
about his widowed bride,
But something touched me deep inside
The day the music died.

Chorus
So bye-bye, Miss American Pie,
Drove my chevy to the levee but the
levee was dry.
Them good old boys were drinkin'
whiskey and rye
Singing, 'This'll be the day that I die,
This'll be the day that I die.'

Verse 2
Did you write the Book of Love,
And do you have faith in God above
If the Bible tells you so?
Do you believe in rock 'n roll,
Can music save your mortal soul,
And can you teach me how to dance real
slow?
Well, I know that you're in love with him
'Cause I saw you dancing in the gym:
You both kicked off your shoes.
Man, I dig those rhythm and blues.
I was a lonely teenage broncing buck
With a pink carnation and a pickup truck
But I knew I was out of luck
The day the music died.
I started singing ...

Chorus

Verse 3
Now for ten years we've been on our
own
And moss grows fat on a rolling stone
But that's not how it used to be.
When the jester sang for the King and
Queen
In a coat he borrowed from James Dean
And a voice that came from you and me.
Oh, and while the King was looking
down
The jester stole his thorny crown.
The courtroom was adjourned,
No verdict was returned.
And while Lennon read a book of Marx
The quartet practiced in the park,
And we sang dirges in the dark
The day the music died.
We were singing ...

Chorus

Verse 4
Helter Skelter in a summer swelter,
The Byrds flew off with a fallout shelter:
Eight miles high and falling fast.
It landed foul out on the grass,
The players tried for a forward pass
With the jester on the sidelines in a cast.
Now the half-time air was sweet
perfume
While the Sergeants played a marching
tune.
We all got up to dance
Oh, but we never got the chance
'Cause the players tried to take the field,
The marching band refused to yield,
Do you recall what was revealed
The day the music died?
We started singing ...

Chorus

Verse 5
Oh, and there we were all in one place:
A generation lost in space
With no time left to start again.
So come on, Jack be nimble, Jack be
quick,
Jack Flash sat on a candlestick
'Cause fire is the devil's only friend.
Oh, and as I watched him on the stage
My hands were clenched in fists of rage:
No angel born in hell
Could break that Satan's spell
And as the flames climbed high into the
night
To light the sacrifical rite
I saw Satan laughing with delight
The day the music died.
He was singing ...

Chorus

Verse 6
I met a girl who sang the blues,
And I asked her for some happy news
But she just smiled and turned away.
I went down to the sacred store
Where I'd heard the music years before
But the man there said the music
wouldn't play.
And in the streets the children screamed,
The lovers cried, and the poets dreamed,
But not a word was spoken,
The church bells all were broken.
And the three men I admire most -
The Father, Son and the Holy Ghost -
They caught the last train for the coast
The day the music died.
And they were singing ...

Chorus

The Complete Rock & Pop Guitar Player
Part 2

INTRODUCTION

This is the second part in *The Complete Rock & Pop Guitar Player* course. As before, all the songs you will learn to play have been big hits for well-known artists.

By following strum patterns in **Part 1** you will already be accustomed to learning songs in this format. **Part 2** features more strumming patterns and some new chords. But it has an extra feature. Some of the songs have short musical examples written in standard notation and guitar-friendly TAB. A fretboard diagram showing the location of all the notes is included.

Full lyrics are included on pages 88-93.
The songs have been graded; each one introduces new chords, strum patterns or necessary revision of what you have already learnt.

As with all parts of this course, it is suitable for use with or without a teacher. All the musical examples are recorded for you on the CD for Part 2, first with the simple guitar strum, and then without as a backing track for you to play along with.

BLUE SUEDE SHOES
Words & Music by Carl Lee Perkins

A9 Chord

D9 Chord

Elvis Presley

'**B**lue Suede Shoes' was an early hit for Elvis in 1956. It's another example of a rock'n'roll 12-bar but with some new chord substitutions. In Part 1 you saw how a 12-bar could be played with A, D, and E.

You also learned the shapes for **D7** and **E7** which can be substituted for the simple **D** or **E major** to add a bit more 'colour'. The next step is to try the ninth chord.

These five note chords are extensions of sevenths like **D7**, **C7**, **B7**, and are often heard in rock'n'roll and blues music. To get **E9** simply move the **D9** shape up **two frets**.

Notice how on the intro you only strum intermittently in the places indicated. The steady strum does not begin until the **D9** and even so it has more 'spaces' in it than some of the songs you have learned.

Before you start, make sure that you're in tune with CD2. Tuning notes for each string are supplied on **Track 1**.

2 BAR CLICK INTRO

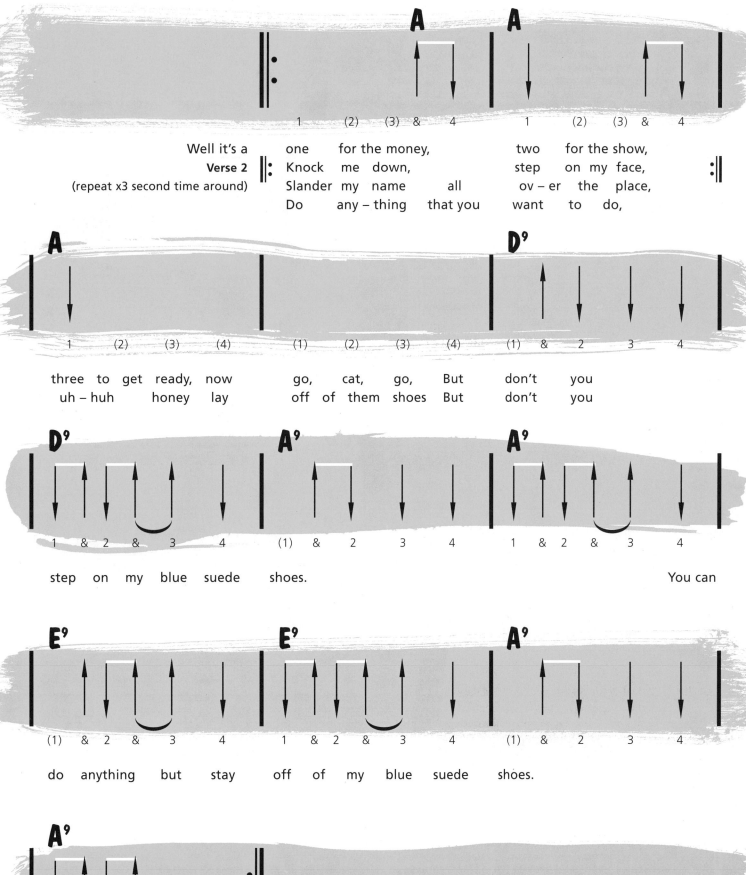

Well it's a one for the money, two for the show,

Verse 2 Knock me down, step on my face,

(repeat x3 second time around) Slander my name all ov – er the place,

Do any – thing that you want to do,

three to get ready, now go, cat, go, But don't you

uh – huh honey lay off of them shoes But don't you

step on my blue suede shoes. You can

do anything but stay off of my blue suede shoes.

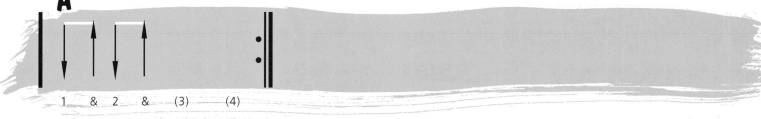

2. Well you can

DRIFTWOOD
Words & Music by Fran Healy

This ambient ballad by Travis gets part of its sound from the fact that the acoustic guitar on the original is played with a capo at the 7th fret. So to play along with the CD backing track you will need to do the same.

This song requires two new chords: **Asus4** and **G6** - both easy shapes!

In the **Asus4** chord one of the original three notes of **A major** has been replaced by another, the fourth of the scale. '**Sus**' is short for '**suspended**'. You can find out more about the way chords are made in Part 3. For the moment all you need to know is that this **Asus4** is neither major nor minor. Notice it has a tense quality.

Fran Healy (Travis)

Asus4 Chord

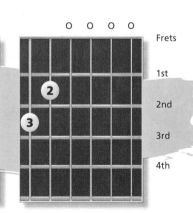

G6 Chord

For the chorus of '**Driftwood**' you can try a continuous 16th note strum. This means going down and up twice on each beat, instead of once for 8ths. It is more usual to find 16ths used occasionally because they get quite tiring to play, and also because they only really work at slow to medium speeds. If you wish, you can play 16ths throughout the whole song. To improve the sound of a 16th note strum use a thin pick and brush the strings lightly up and down.

2 BAR CLICK + 4 BAR INTRO

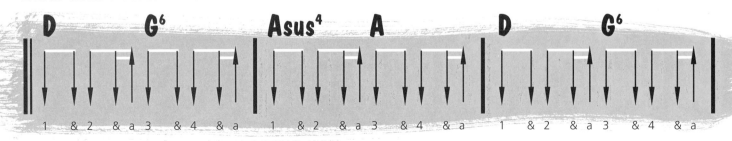

| D | G6 | Asus4 | A | D | G6 |

1 & 2 & a 3 & 4 & a   1 & 2 & a 3 & 4 & a   1 & 2 & a 3 & 4 & a

Ev - ery thing is op - en,   nothing is set in stone.   Rivers turn to oceans,

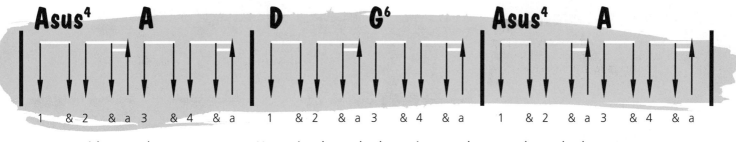

Asus⁴ **A**   **D** **G⁶**   **Asus⁴** **A**

1 & 2 & a 3 & 4 & a   1 & 2 & a 3 & 4 & a   1 & 2 & a 3 & 4 & a

oceans tide you home.   Home is where the heart is,   but your heart had to roam.

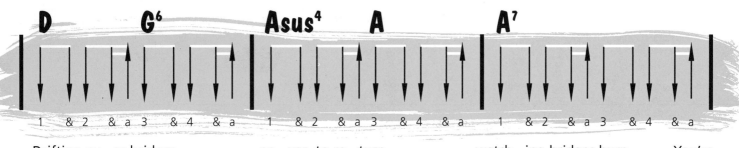

D **G⁶**   **Asus⁴** **A**   **A⁷**

1 & 2 & a 3 & 4 & a   1 & 2 & a 3 & 4 & a   1 & 2 & a 3 & 4 & a

Drifting ov - er bridges   ne - ver to re - turn,   watch - ing bridges burn.   You're

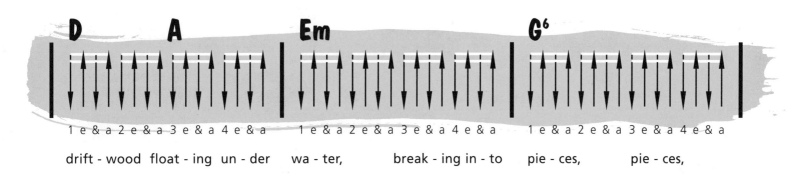

D **A**   **Em**   **G⁶**

1 e & a 2 e & a 3 e & a 4 e & a   1 e & a 2 e & a 3 e & a 4 e & a   1 e & a 2 e & a 3 e & a 4 e & a

drift - wood float - ing un - der   wa - ter,   break - ing in - to   pie - ces,   pie - ces,

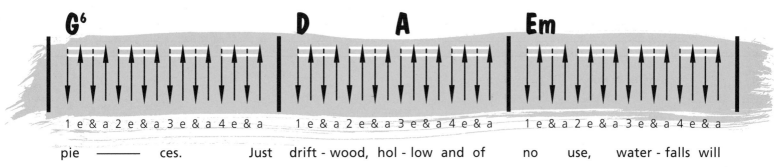

G⁶   **D** **A**   **Em**

1 e & a 2 e & a 3 e & a 4 e & a   1 e & a 2 e & a 3 e & a 4 e & a   1 e & a 2 e & a 3 e & a 4 e & a

pie ——— ces.   Just   drift - wood, hol - low and of   no   use,   water - falls will

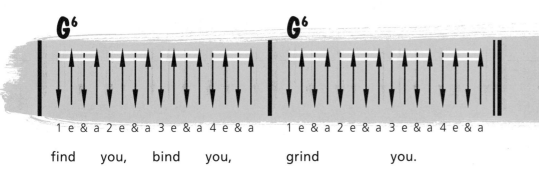

G⁶   **G⁶**

1 e & a 2 e & a 3 e & a 4 e & a   1 e & a 2 e & a 3 e & a 4 e & a

find   you,   bind   you,   grind   you.

David Gray

SAIL AWAY
Words & Music by David Gray

Bmadd¹¹ Chord

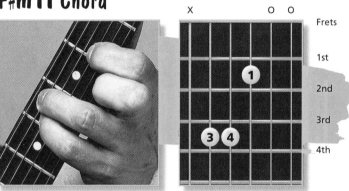

This recent hit for David Gray introduces a new idea you can apply to the chord shapes you have learned.

These two chords are derived from the **F#m** chord shape you met in Part 1. What has happened is that the barre has been taken off, the first finger has gone to the 3rd string and the 6th string is not played.

This song features a new, complicated off-beat strumming pattern for you to learn. The best way to do this is to listen to the demonstration track and try and 'feel' the rhythm. The other way to learn it is by slowing it right down and counting. Here's how it should go:

F#m 11 Chord

Only count, or play, the bold notes. It looks complicated, but slow it right down and you should get the feel of the rhythm. Then, gradually speed it up.

If you can't manage this you can always play any of the other 4/4 rhythm patterns you've learnt. Just try and pick one that would fit the feel of this song.

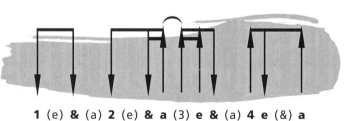

1 (e) **&** (a) **2** (e) **& a** (3) e **&** (a) **4** e (**&**) **a**

CAPO 1ST FRET
1 BAR CLICK + 4 BAR INTRO

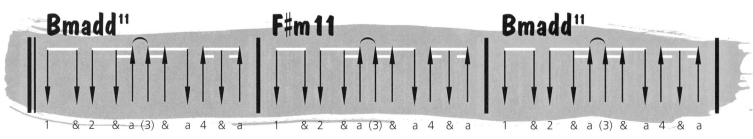

Bmadd¹¹   **F#m 11**   **Bmadd¹¹**

1 & 2 & a (3) & a 4 & a   1 & 2 & a (3) & a 4 & a   1 & 2 & a (3) & a 4 & a

Sail a - way with me honey,   I put my heart in your hands.   Sail a - way with me honey,

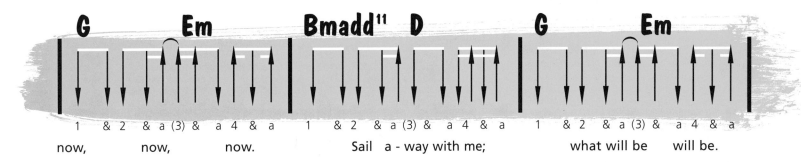

G   **Em**   **Bmadd¹¹**   **D**   **G**   **Em**

1 & 2 & a (3) & a 4 & a   1 & 2 & a (3) & a 4 & a   1 & 2 & a (3) & a 4 & a

now,   now,   now.   Sail a - way with me;   what will be   will be.

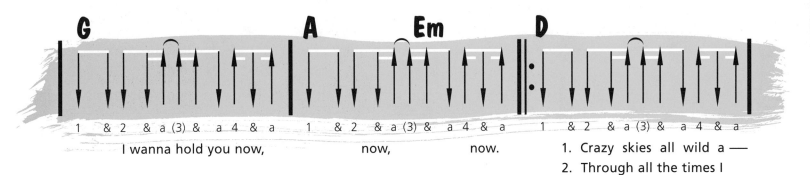

G   **A**   **Em**   **D**

1 & 2 & a (3) & a 4 & a   1 & 2 & a (3) & a 4 & a   1 & 2 & a (3) & a 4 & a

I wanna hold you now,   now,   now.   1. Crazy skies all wild a —
     2. Through all the times I

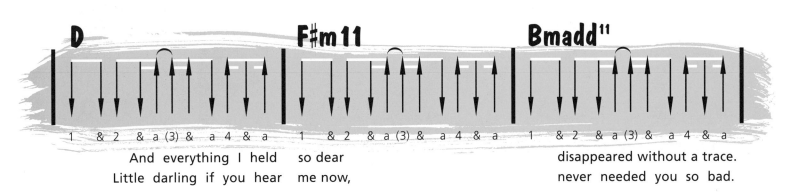

F#m11   **D**   **F#m11**

1 & 2 & a (3) & a 4 & a   1 & 2 & a (3) & a 4 & a   1 & 2 & a (3) & a 4 & a

— bove me now,   winter howling at my face.
tast - ed love,   never knew quite what I had.

D   **F#m11**   **Bmadd¹¹**

1 & 2 & a (3) & a 4 & a   1 & 2 & a (3) & a 4 & a   1 & 2 & a (3) & a 4 & a

And everything I held   so dear   disappeared without a trace.
Little darling if you hear   me now,   never needed you so bad.

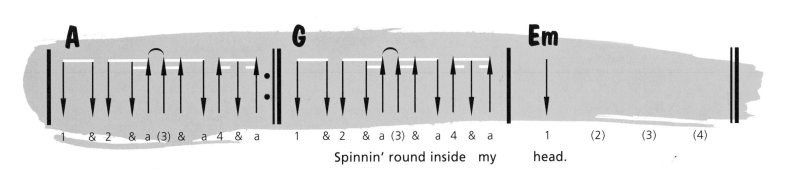

A   **G**   **Em**

1 & 2 & a (3) & a 4 & a   1 & 2 & a (3) & a 4 & a   1 (2) (3) (4)

     Spinnin' round inside my   head.

WILD WOOD
Words & Music by Paul Weller

F#m/B Chord

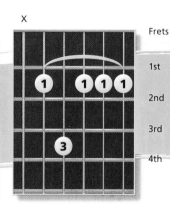

Em7 Chord

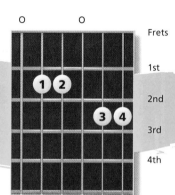

This 1993 hit by Paul Weller has a relaxed acoustic feel that is quite easy to reproduce. There are three new chord shapes for you.

The **Em7** is a less common shape for this chord than the **Em7** you learned in Book One, but makes more sense harmonically for this song. The **F#7#5♭9** is an even rarer chord and helps to give '**Wild Wood**' its slightly jazzy quality.

F#7#5♭9 Chord

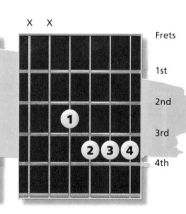

The **Bm** chord is the standard **Bm barre** shape and can be played by using the **C#m** shape in Part 1 moved down two frets.

With the strumming watch out for the quick up and down that comes on the last beat of the bar.

Paul Weller

1 BAR CLICK + 4 BAR INTRO

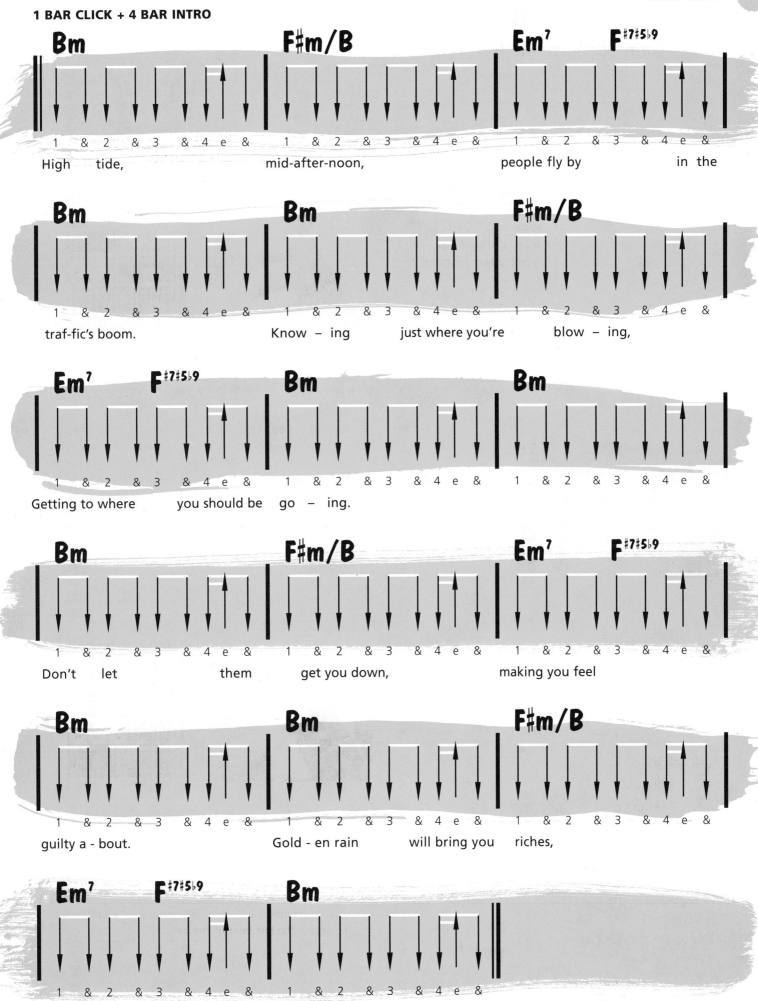

ROLL WITH IT
Words & Music by Noel Gallagher

'Roll With It' was one of several hit singles taken from Oasis' huge album *(What's The Story) Morning Glory?* (1995). It is a good example of how effective chord changes can be made by adapting a few shapes, and how you can adapt shapes so you don't always need to move all your fingers.

For this song we need four new shapes: **A7**, **C7**, **Cadd9** and **G/B**, which are pretty simple, straightforward open chords. The seventh chords give the intro a hard, no-nonsense rock sound.

Cadd9 Chord

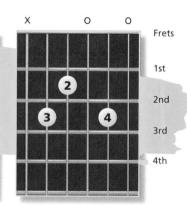

A7 Chord

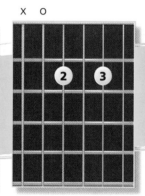

C7 Chord

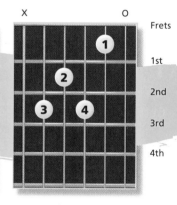

G/B Chord

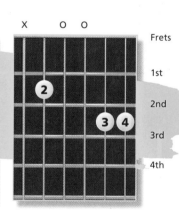

Most of the strumming in 'Roll With It' is straight 8ths, with examples of omitted off-beat strums from time to time.

These little variations help to make your strumming more interesting than if you played 8ths all the time. Letting a chord ring for a beat or two, or coming back in on an offbeat are some of the ways of making rhythms more interesting.

1 BAR CLICK INTRO

D7   C7   1.2.   G

1 2 (3) & 4 &   1 2 (3) & 4 &   1 2 3 & 4 &

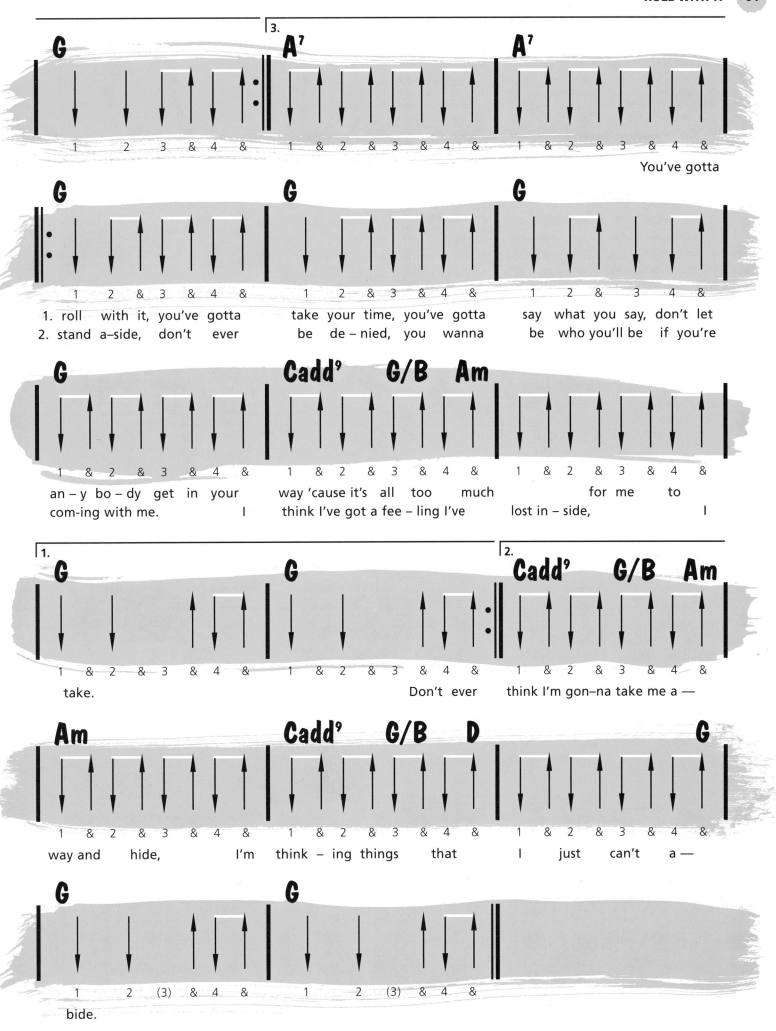

TRACK
12+13
CD2

20TH CENTURY BOY
Words & Music by Marc Bolan

© Copyright 1973 Wizard (Bahamas) Limited.
All Rights Reserved. International Copyright Secured.

This classic slice of glam rock was a hit for T.Rex first in 1973, then in 1991 after use on a Levi's commercial, and also featured on the soundtrack of the film *Billy Elliot*. '20th Century Boy' uses the chords E, A and B - all of which you have played before.

The strum for '**20th Century Boy**' is mostly 8ths. Watch out for the 8th/16th/16th figure on the last beat of bar 2, which can also be found elsewhere in the song. You can also try learning the song's famous riff (see tab below).

The arrow indicates that the 2nd fret (**F♯**) on the bottom **E** string is bent a semitone, and is called a semitone, or half-tone bend. To play this, bend push the string upwards quickly after striking the note.

Marc Bolan (T.Rex)

Here is the song's opening guitar riff:

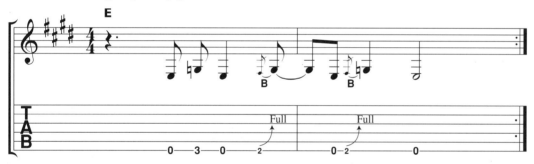

2 BAR CLICK + 2 BAR INTRO

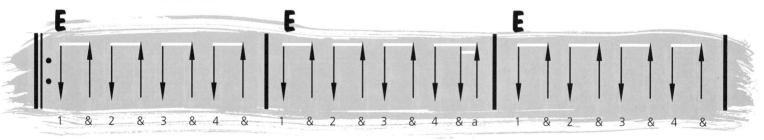

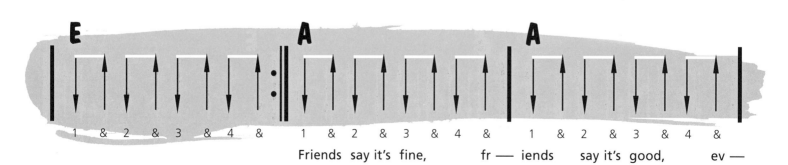

Friends say it's fine,   fr — iends   say it's good,   ev —

62

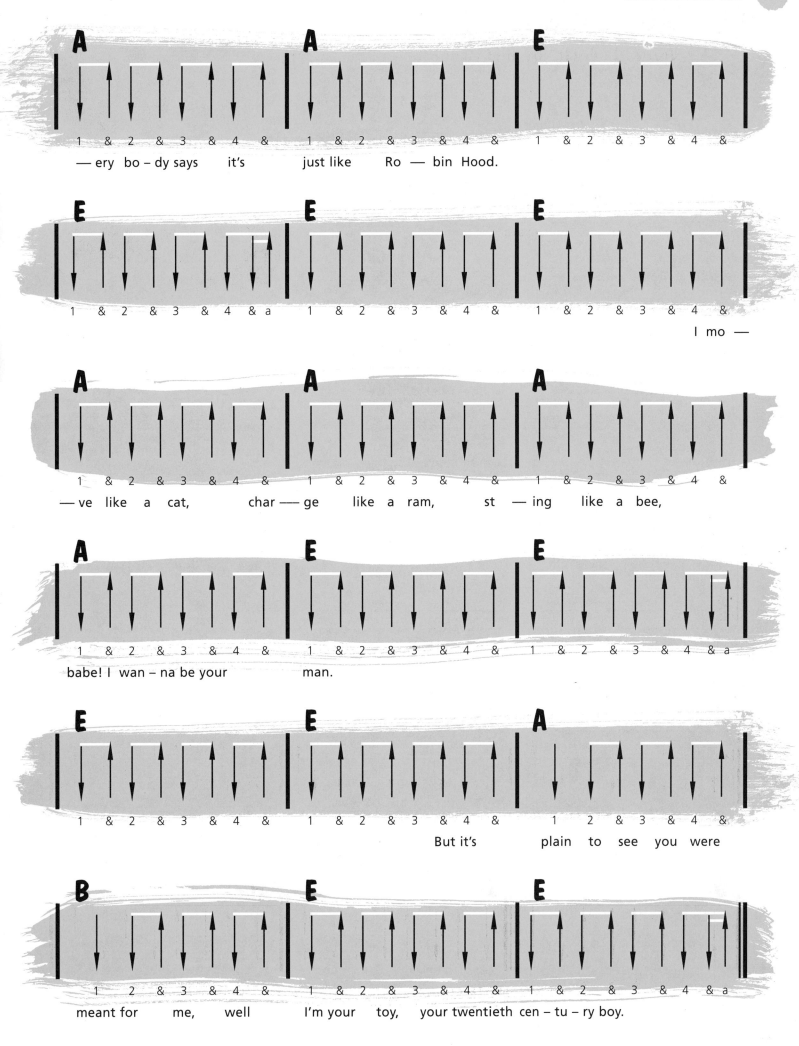

SHE LOVES YOU
Words & Music by John Lennon & Paul McCartney

This great example of the early 'Fab Four'
features the chords G, Em, Bm, D, D7 and A,
all of which you know. The Cm can be played
by taking the Bm from 'Wild Wood' and
moving it up one fret.

'She Loves You' has two famous guitar fills. Here they are:

GUITAR FILL 1

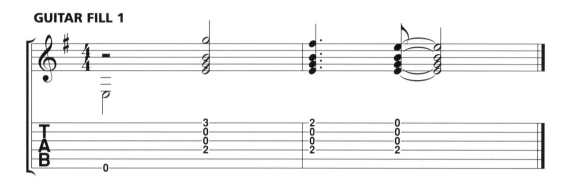

GUITAR FILL 2

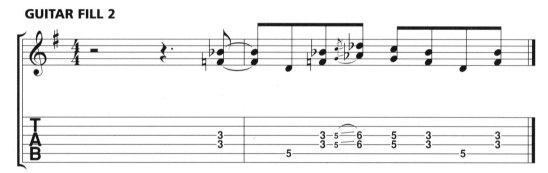

CAPO 1ST FRET
2 BAR CLICK + 8 BAR INTRO

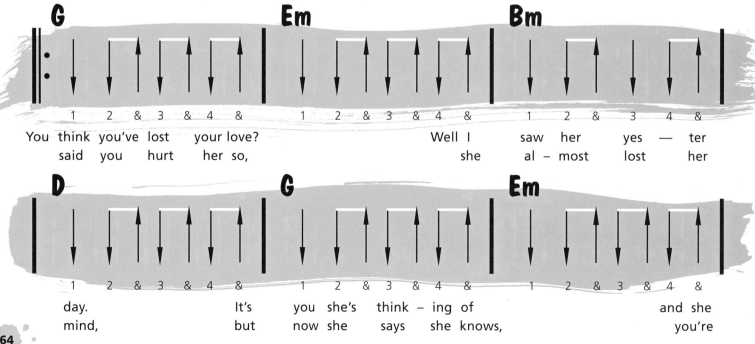

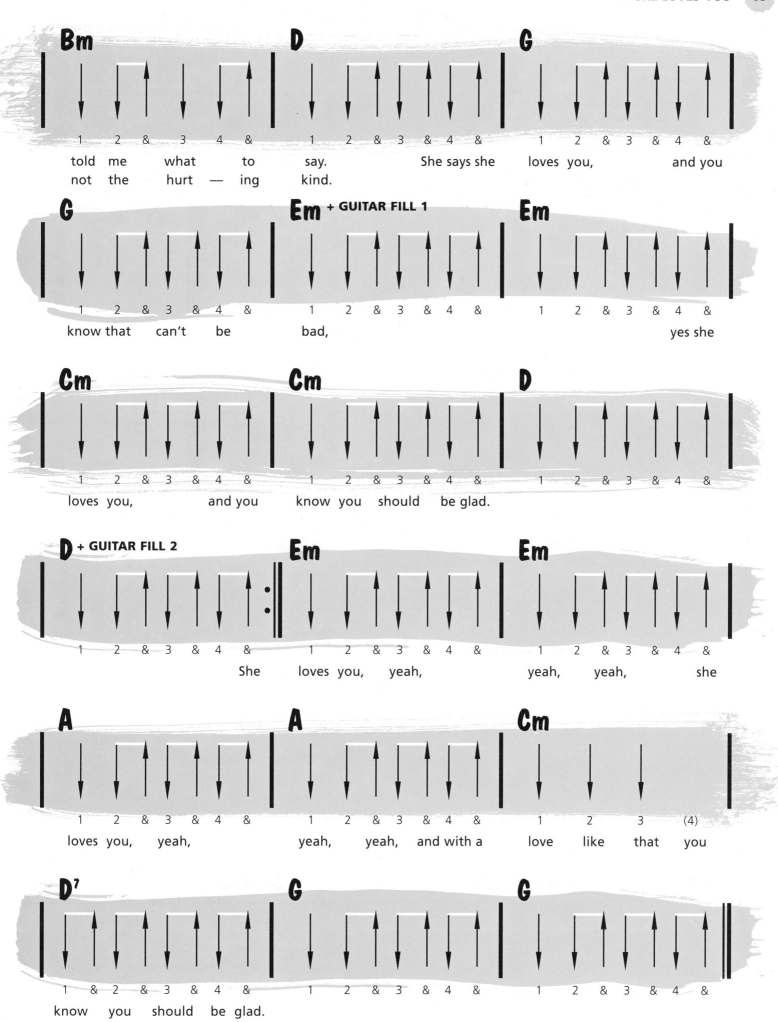

I SHOT THE SHERIFF
Words & Music by Bob Marley

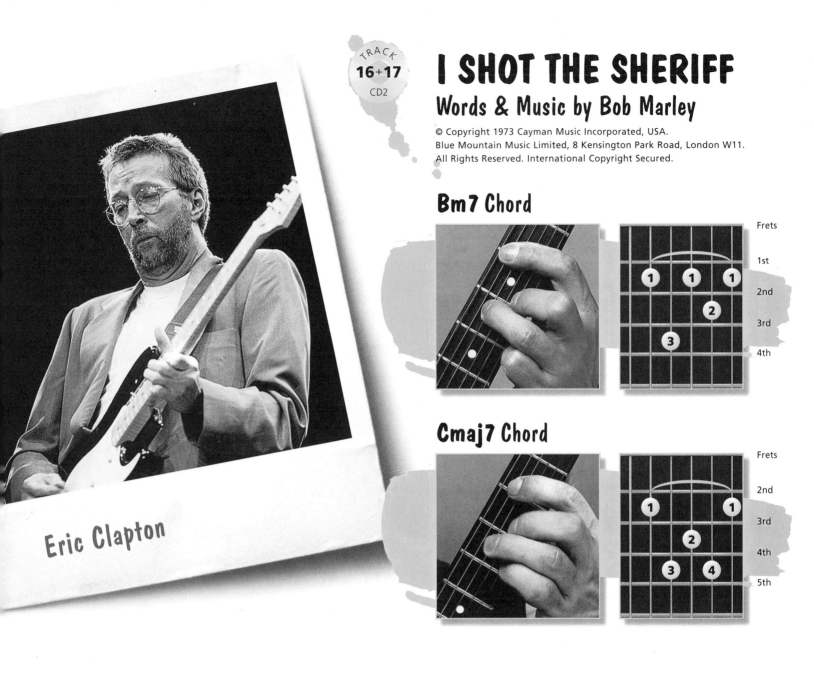

Eric Clapton

Bm7 Chord

Cmaj7 Chord

Eric Clapton had a smash hit with this Bob Marley song in 1974.

This song has a reggae feel due to the fact that you strum on the 'off-beats' of the bar – the 2nd and 4th. Watch out for the rhythm change from the chorus to the verse.

There are two new chords, **Bm7** and **Cmaj7** (see above).

Cmaj7 can also be played by holding down a **C** chord and lifting your 1st finger off the 2nd string. However this barre version sounds better here and makes the change to **Bm7** easier (both barred and the third finger is a guide finger).

To play along with the CD simply put a capo on at the third fret. This will put you in the right key as the original without changing any of the riff fingering or the chord shapes.

**CAPO 3RD FRET
1 BAR CLICK INTRO**

CHORUS

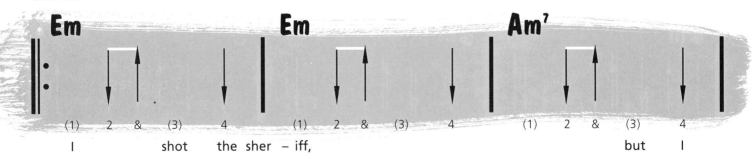

Em				Em				Am⁷			
(1)	2	&	(3)	4	(1)	2	&	(3)	4	(1)	2	&	(3)	4
I		shot	the sher – iff,							but	I

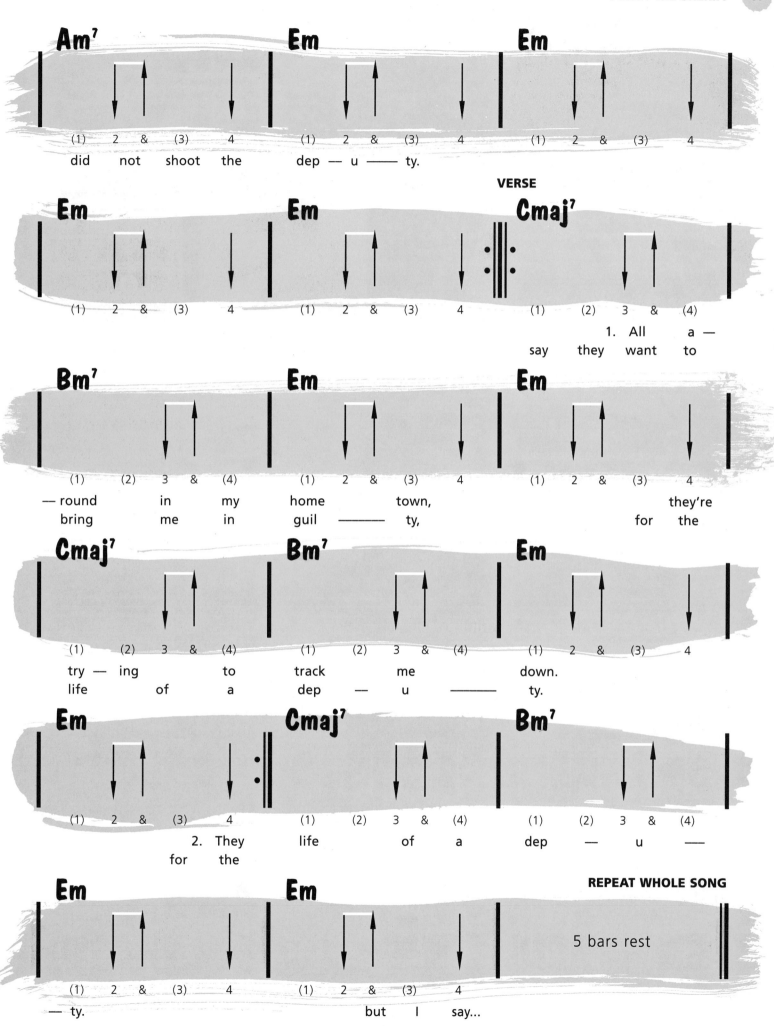

SUNNY AFTERNOON
Words & Music by Ray Davies

Dm Chord

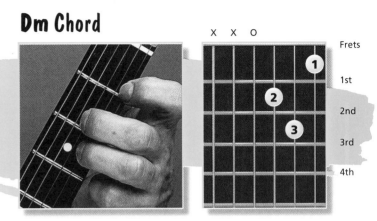

To play The Kinks' No.1 from the summer of 1966 you will need one new chord, D minor:

Along with **Am** and **Em**, **Dm** is the most popular of the open string minor shapes. It isn't as full-sounding as the other two because the root note is only as low as the open fourth string and only four strings are played.

'**Sunny Afternoon**' gets some of its jaunty feel from the fact that the rhythm is lightly swung. As with '**Rock Around The Clock**' this means that the pairs of 8ths are not even in length. Each beat feels as though it is dividing into three. So tap the beat, count 1,2,3, and make your down strum last for 1,2, and your up strum falls on the '3'.

When you are working out how to do a chord change always look to see if there is a guide finger. This is a finger that either moves up or down the same string or doesn't move at all. So if you change from **C** to **F (full barre)** there is no need for the 3rd finger to move. If you change from **A** to **Dm** there is no need for the 2nd finger to move. If you notice these sorts of fingerings you will find chord changing quicker.

Here is the **DESCENDING BASS FIGURE** that starts the song:

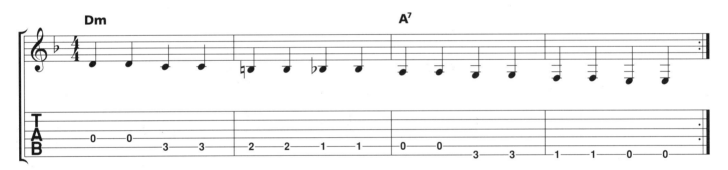

2 BAR CLICK + 8 BAR INTRO

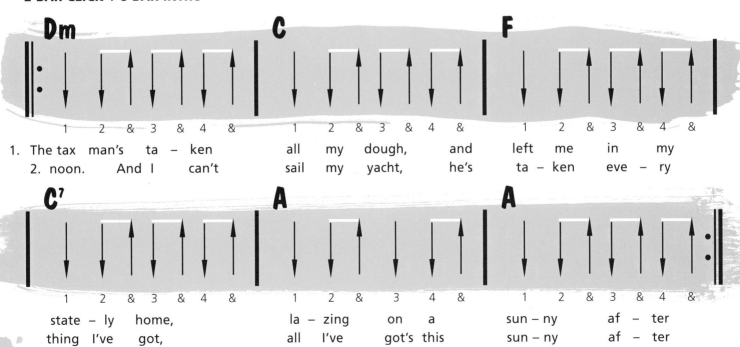

1. The tax man's ta – ken   all   my   dough,   and   left   me   in   my
2. noon.   And I   can't   sail   my   yacht,   he's   ta – ken   eve – ry

state – ly   home,   la – zing   on   a   sun – ny   af – ter
thing I've   got,   all I've   got's this   sun – ny   af – ter

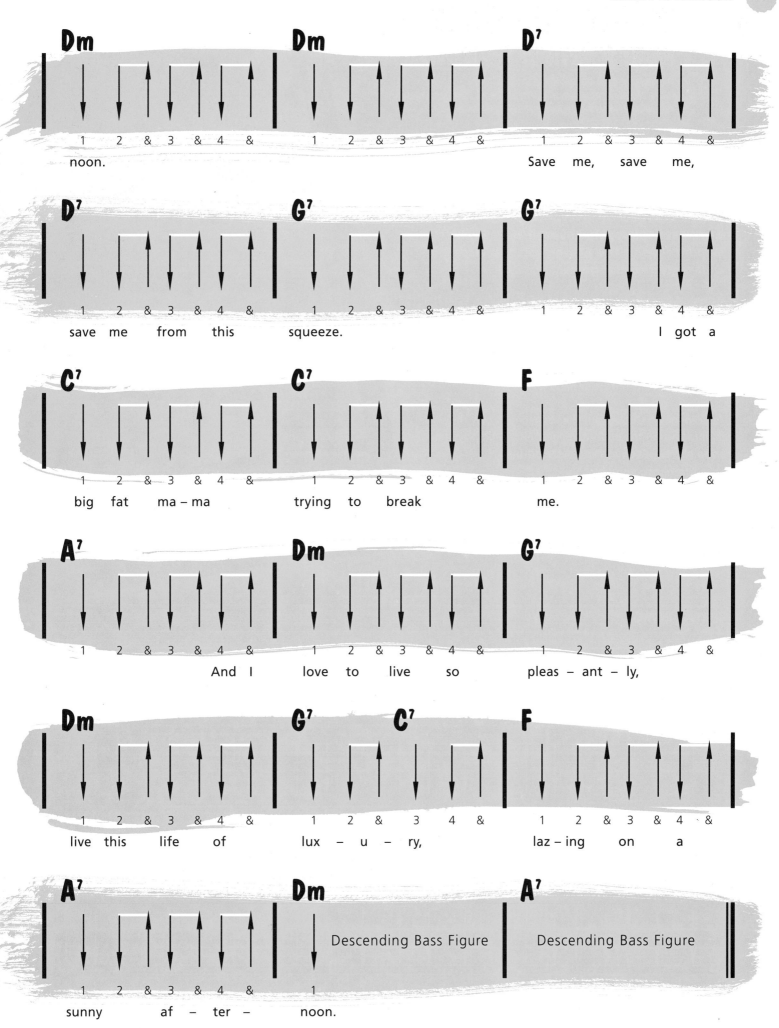

THERE SHE GOES
Words & Music by Lee Mavers

First recorded by Liverpool group The La's and subsequently covered by U.S. outfit Sixpence None The Richer, this 90s classic is well-suited to the guitar.

The famous chiming guitar figure on the intro is easy to play once you get the hang of the rhythm. When picking the top two strings use alternating down and up strokes with the pick. Unlike strumming, picking single notes requires only a small movement; your arm and even much of your hand will be still.

You can play it throughout the song, or just play the rhythm part on the opposite page. This can be played with a straight-eighth strumming pattern.

The La's

GUITAR INTRO

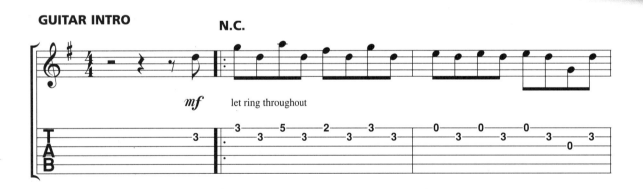

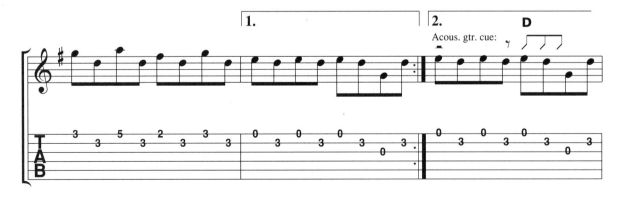

4 BAR INTRO

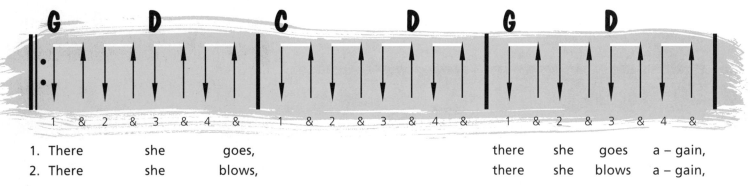

1. There　　she　　goes,　　　　　　　there　she　goes　a – gain,
2. There　　she　　blows,　　　　　　　there　she　blows　a – gain,

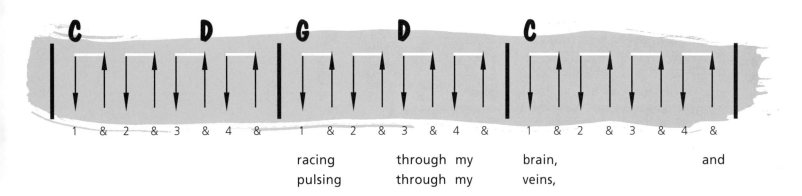

racing　　through　my　brain,　　　　　　and
pulsing　through　my　veins,

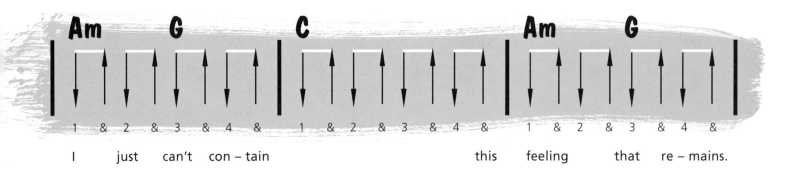

I　just　can't　con – tain　　　　　　this　feeling　that　re – mains.

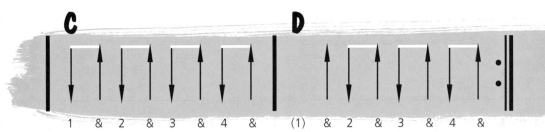

HEY JOE
Words & Music by William M. Roberts

The entire song here is based on a single four-bar chord progression using C, G, D, A, E and E7. Notice the first is the tie sign (⌒) used to tie two notes of the same pitch together so that only the first of the tied notes is played. You can see this in bar 3 of 'Hey Joe'.

To play this bar strum all the marks as shown but leave out the one that falls directly over the 4, letting the previous strum (a chord change to **E7**) ring instead.

You can also try your hand at this catchy chromatic riff which fits perfectly under the chords and is instantly recognisable as the famous bass riff from the Jimi Hendrix smash hit recording of this song.

A chromatic phrase is one which uses notes that are not properly in key. Chromatic phrases usually feature lots of semitone movement in either direction. The timing is easy because the riff is a straight eight pattern. Practise it very slowly and evenly before attempting to play it at the correct tempo.

Jimi Hendrix

Here is the main guitar riff:

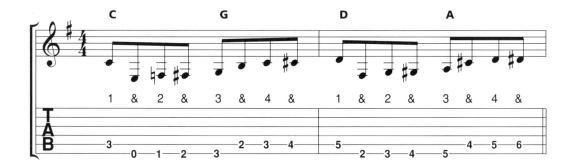

1 BAR CLICK + 3 BAR INTRO

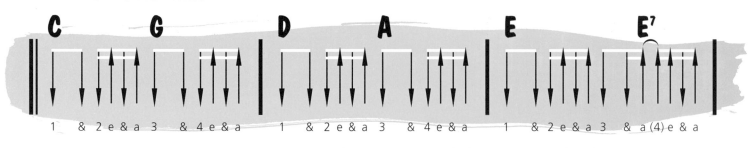

Hey   Joe,   where you goin' with that gun in your hand?

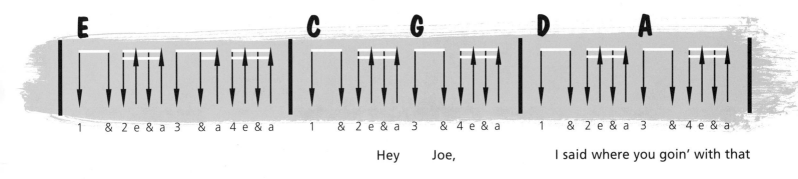

Hey   Joe,   I said where you goin' with that

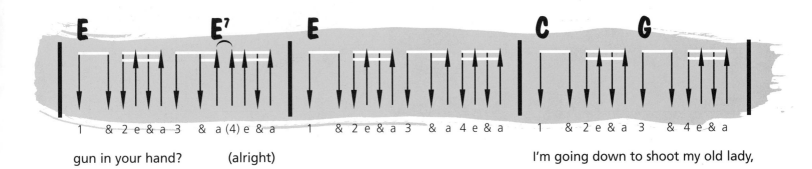

gun in your hand?   (alright)   I'm going down to shoot my old lady,

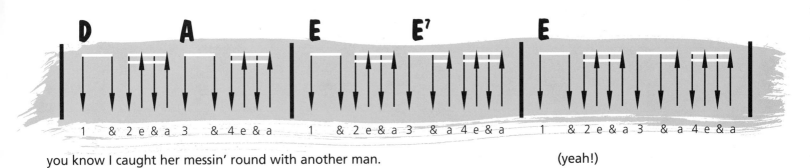

you know I caught her messin' round with another man.   (yeah!)

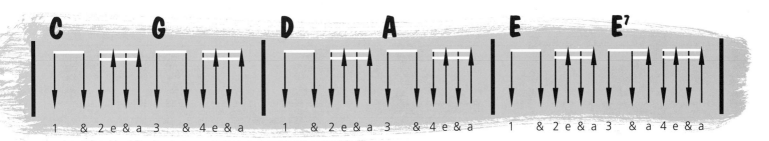

I'm going down to shoot my old lady, you know I caught her messin' round with another man. Huh! And that ain't

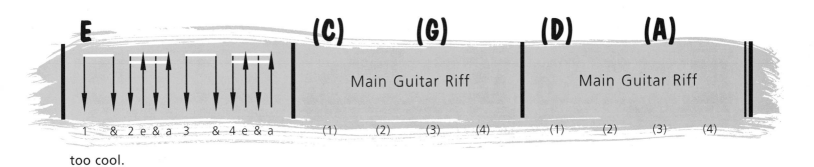

too cool.

Free

ALL RIGHT NOW

Words & Music by Paul Rodgers & Andy Fraser

Dadd9 Chord

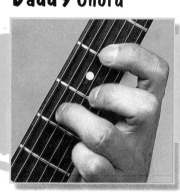
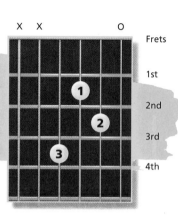

Rock songs don't come much bigger than Free's 'All Right Now', a hit in 1970, 1973 and 1991. Although the song only uses three basic chords - A, D and G, variations on these chords are needed to make what you play sound closer to the original.

Don't worry if you happen to hit the open **A** string under the **Dadd9** chord, it will sound okay. To make the **Dadd9/A** chord, simply strum from the A string instead of from the D.

These chord shapes are suitable for strumming on an acoustic. In the verse there are a number of beats where you need to damp the strings altogether when you hit them

(these are beats marked with a 'x'). Watch out for the 'anticipated' chords in the chorus, played on the last offbeat of the bar and tied across into the next bar.

On the second time you play the chorus, watch out for the final A chord – the timing is different. You need to play it on beat 1 of the last bar, rather than beat 4 of the previous bar, so it doesn't sound 'anticipated'.

If you want to try the verse and chorus riffs as they are played on electric guitar, here they are in TAB:

VERSE & INTRO RIFF

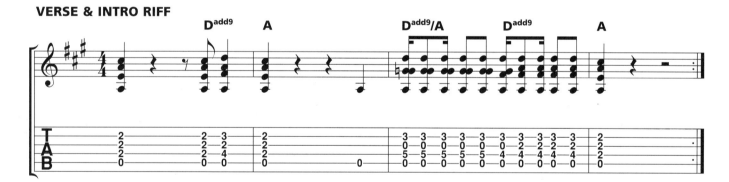

CHORUS RIFF

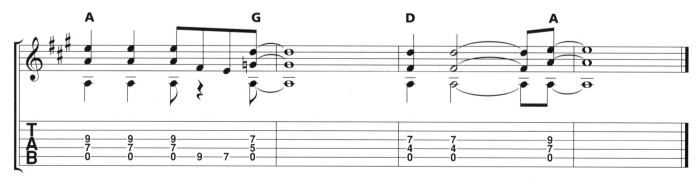

**2 BAR CLICK + 8 BAR INTRO
(SEE VERSE & INTRO RIFF)**

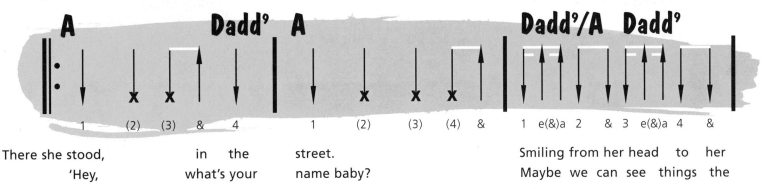

There she stood,   in the   street.   Smiling from her head   to   her
'Hey,   what's your   name baby?   Maybe we can see things the

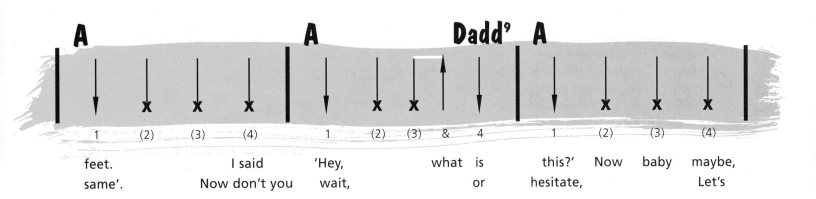

feet.   I said   'Hey,   what is   this?' Now   baby   maybe,
same'.   Now don't you   wait,   or   hesitate,   Let's

CHORUS RIFF

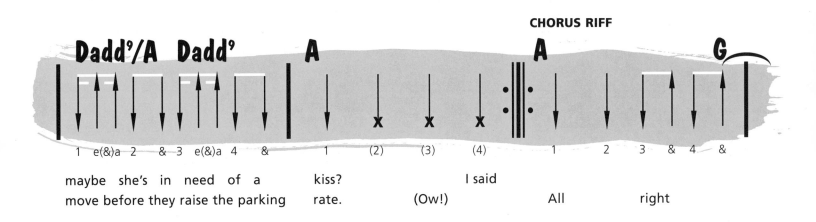

maybe she's in need of a   kiss?   I said   All   right
move before they raise the parking   rate.   (Ow!)

2nd time play on 1st beat only

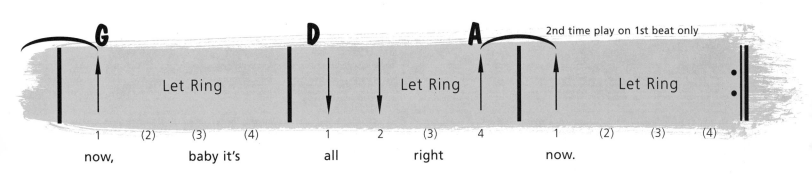

now,   baby it's   all   right   now.

NIGHTS IN WHITE SATIN
Words & Music by Justin Hayward

Taken from their concept album *Days Of Future Passed*, this romantic ballad charted for The Moody Blues on no less than three occasions, in 1967, 1972 and 1979, and uses a new time-signature: 6/8.

This basically means that there are six quavers in each bar, as opposed to the four crotchets you are used to. 6/8 has a kind of lilting rhythm and is commonly used for ballads.

If you're wondering what the difference is between 6/8 and 3/4 (as they both basically add up to the same number of beats), it is simply that you can 'feel' **two** main beats in each bar of 6/8 (each beat made up of three quavers), whereas in 3/4 it is definitely **three** main beats (each beat made up of two quavers). It is a subtle difference but see if you can spot it.

For more on time signatures, see page 84.

When you have mastered the chord changes and strumming pattern for this song, why not try learning the flute solo as well? We've arranged it for guitar, below:

The Moody Blues

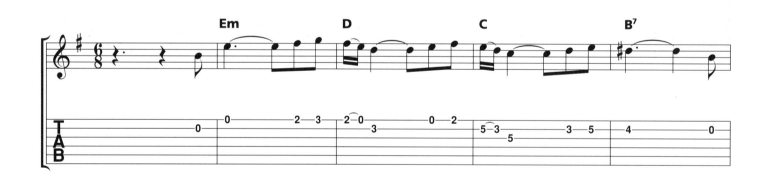

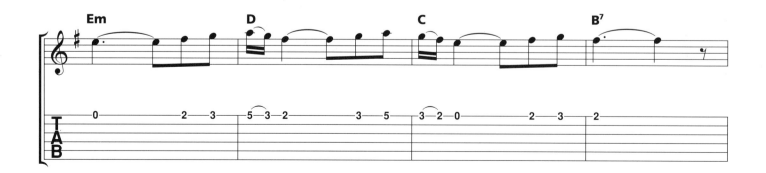

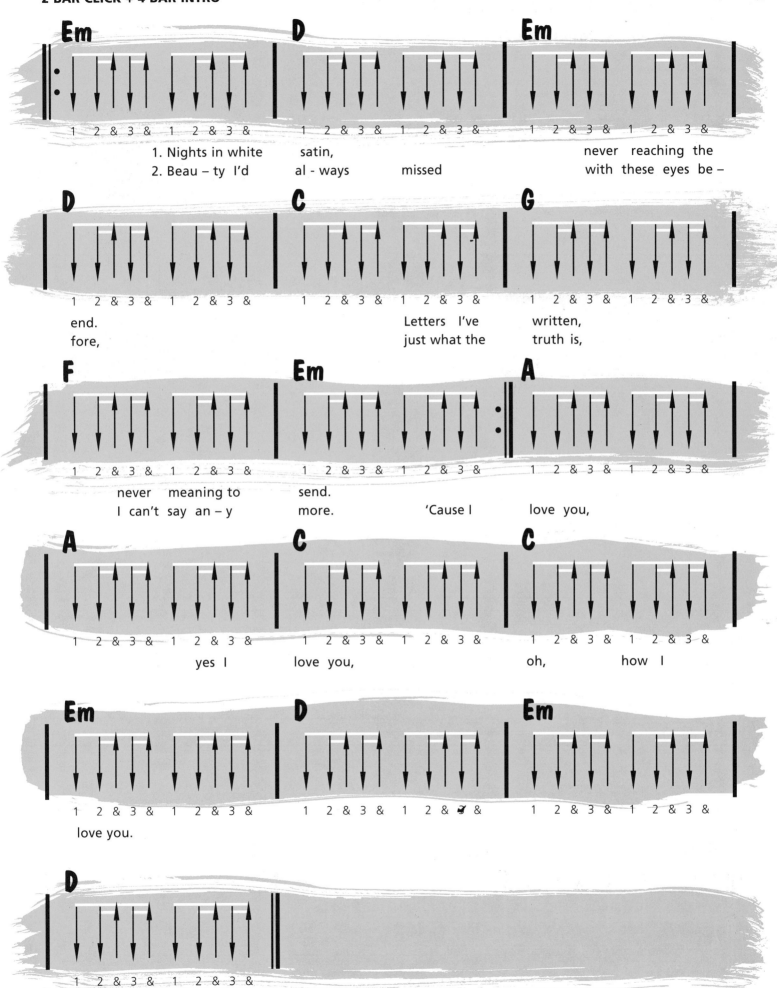

Em
1 2 & 3 & 1 2 & 3 &
1. Nights in white   satin,
2. Beau – ty I'd   al - ways   missed

D
1 2 & 3 & 1 2 & 3 &

Em
1 2 & 3 & 1 2 & 3 &
never reaching the
with these eyes be –

D
1 2 & 3 & 1 2 & 3 &
end.
fore,

C
1 2 & 3 & 1 2 & 3 &
Letters I've
just what the

G
1 2 & 3 & 1 2 & 3 &
written,
truth is,

F
1 2 & 3 & 1 2 & 3 &
never   meaning to
I can't say an – y

Em
1 2 & 3 & 1 2 & 3 &
send.
more.

A
1 2 & 3 & 1 2 & 3 &
'Cause I   love you,

A
1 2 & 3 & 1 2 & 3 &
yes I

C
1 2 & 3 & 1 2 & 3 &
love you,

C
1 2 & 3 & 1 2 & 3 &
oh,   how I

Em
1 2 & 3 & 1 2 & 3 &
love you.

D
1 2 & 3 & 1 2 & &

Em
1 2 & 3 & 1 2 & 3 &

D
1 2 & 3 & 1 2 & 3 &

WHILE MY GUITAR GENTLY WEEPS

Words & Music by George Harrison

Am/G Chord

 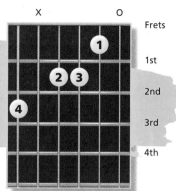

F#m Chord

 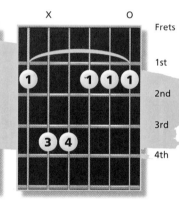

George Harrison

George Harrison's ballad appeared on The Beatles' *White Album*. It introduces one new chord: Am/G.

We could use an **Am7** for this (try it for contrast) but **Am/G** is preferable because it preserves the descending bass line under the chords. The next chord **D/F#** has that bass-line moving down one more semitone. The **F#m** in the bridge is an Fm shape moved up one fret.

The strumming is straight 8ths in the verse, but watch out for the tied 2nd offbeat in the Bridge.

This Bridge also happens to be in a different key. The song starts in **A minor** but changes into **A major**. This is why the mood seems to change at that point.

8 BAR INTRO
VERSE

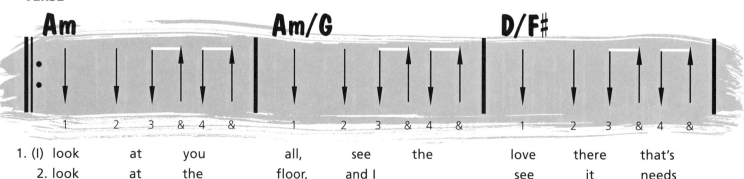

Am					Am/G					D/F#				
1	2	3	& 4	&	1	2	3	& 4	&	1	2	3	& 4	&
1. (I) look	at	you		all,	see	the				love	there	that's		
2. look	at	the		floor,	and I					see	it	needs		

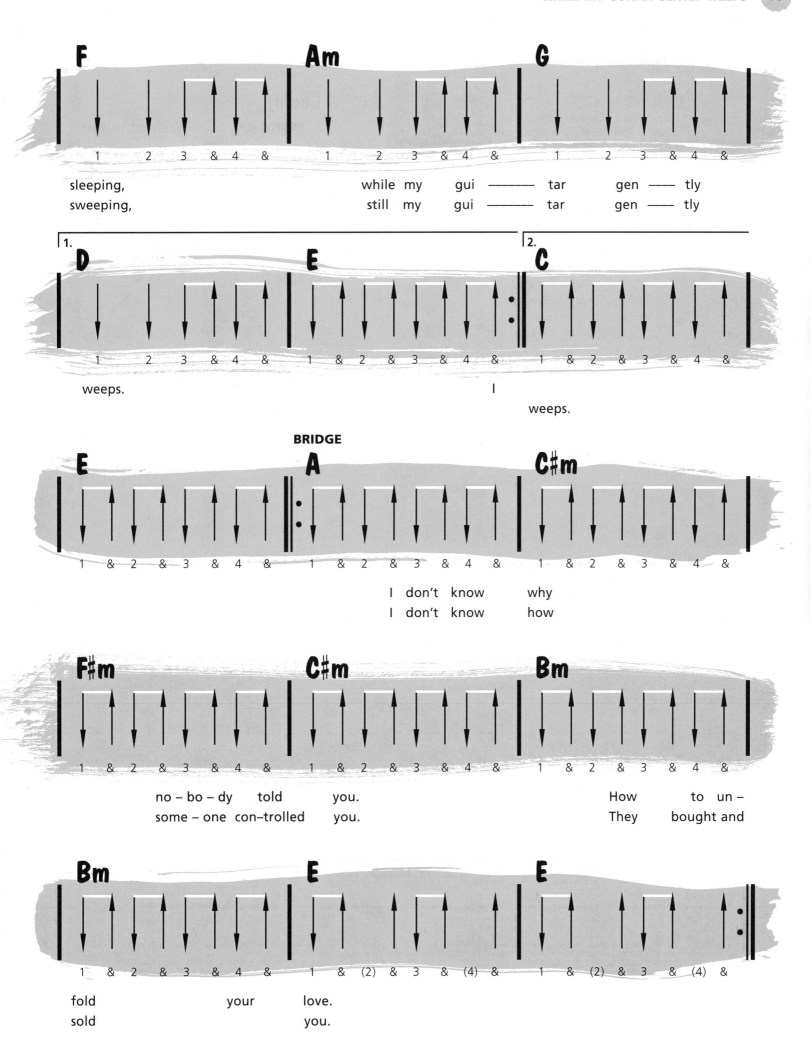

PINBALL WIZARD
Words & Music by
Pete Townshend

Bsus4 / B* Chord

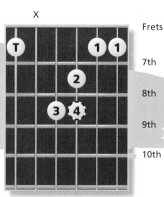

This hit by The Who comes from their rock opera *Tommy*.

You are already familiar with **sus4** chords, but for this song, we're going to have to take it up a few frets, to the 7th. Look at the chord on the right – **Bsus4/B***. Start with a partial barre at the seventh fret, using your first finger. To get the bass note, you'll need to use your thumb too – a tricky technique that might need some practice. You also need to mute the fifth string with the side of your thumb. Then place your other fingers down. Now, strum fast while adding and removing your little finger at the 9th fret – and you've got the intro to 'Pinball Wizard'!

The strum is also challenging, as it's so fast and also accented in an unusual way. Listen to the CD first, then take a look at the music. See if you can 'feel' where the accents should fall. Alternatively, try counting this rhythm accenting the **1** and not counting the (&):

1 2 3 **1** 2 3 **1** 2 3 **1** 2 3 **1** (&) **2** (&)

Now you've almost got it, but there's also the famous intro to learn. We've written it out in TAB, below. Use down strokes to keep the 8th note **F#** going, playing the chord only once, on the first beat of the bar.

Dsus4 Chord

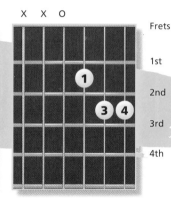

B major Chord

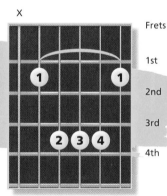

2 BAR CLICK INTRO

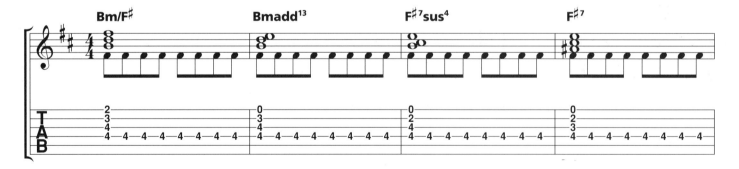

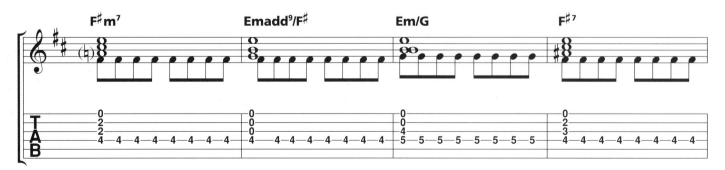

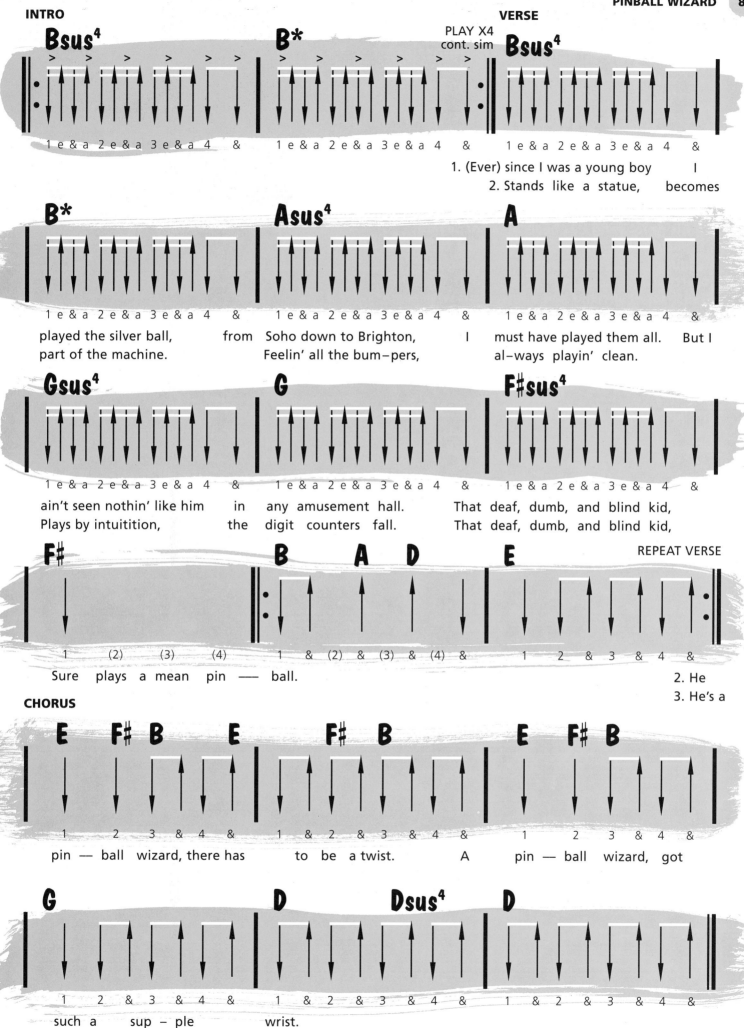

LIGHT MY FIRE

Words & Music by Jim Morrison, Robbie Krieger, Ray Manzarek & John Densmore

Jim Morrison

This great song has been a hit for several performers. The most famous was the original version by The Doors with Jim Morrison on vocals, which charted in 1967 and 1991. Jose Feliciano had a bigger hit with the song in 1968.

When practising minor sevenths play a straight minor version of the chord first, followed by the minor seventh, and listen to the subtle difference in sound.

The **Am7** is simple and needs no explanation, but for the **F♯m7** refer to the **F♯m** shape introduced in '**While My Guitar Gently Weeps**'. Take your little finger off the fourth string. As long as you're careful that your barre (first finger) is pressing down cleanly across the strings you should now be playing **F♯m7**. As this **F♯m7** shape does not use any open strings it is 'moveable'. These two shapes both take their name from the note you are fingering on the sixth string.

That is to say, if:
The tip of your 1st finger is resting on the 2nd fret of the 6th string, the chord is **F♯m7**.

The tip of your 1st finger is resting on the 3rd fret of the 6th string, the chord is **Gm7**.

The tip of your 1st finger is resting on the 4th fret of the 6th string, the chord is **G♯m7**.

Here in TAB is the organ introduction melody.

This is quite fast, so take your time playing it slowly at first and make sure you are using all four fingers to fret these notes.

2 BAR CLICK

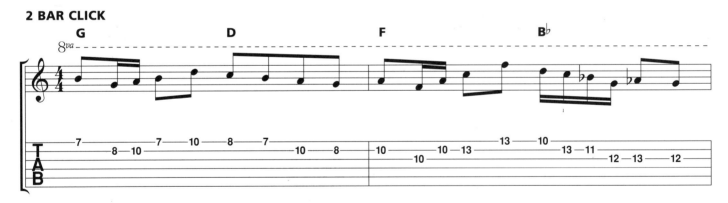

(You)

2 BAR CLICK + 5 BAR INTRO
VERSE

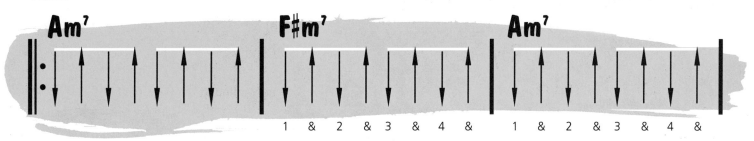

Am⁷   F#m⁷   Am⁷

1 & 2 & 3 & 4 &   1 & 2 & 3 & 4 &

1. (You) know that it would be un – true,   you   know that I would be a li – ar,
time to hes – it – ate is through,   no   time to wallow in the myre.

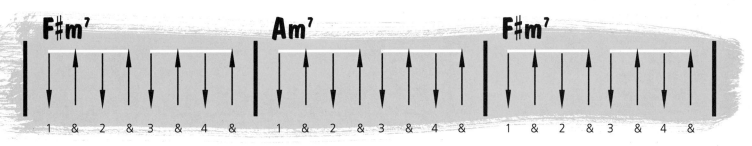

F#m⁷   Am⁷   F#m⁷

1 & 2 & 3 & 4 &   1 & 2 & 3 & 4 &   1 & 2 & 3 & 4 &

If   I   was   to   say   to   you.
Try now, we can on – ly lose.   And our

CHORUS

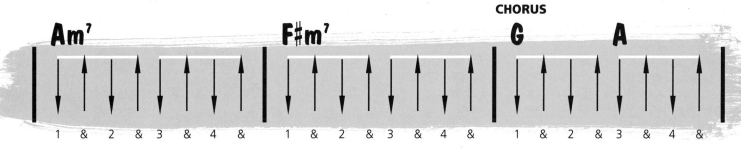

Am⁷   F#m⁷   G   A

1 & 2 & 3 & 4 &   1 & 2 & 3 & 4 &   1 & 2 & 3 & 4 &

Girl, we couldn't get much higher.
love become a funeral pyre.   Come on ba – by, light my fire.

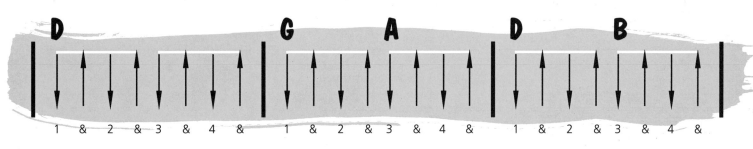

D   G   A   D   B

1 & 2 & 3 & 4 &   1 & 2 & 3 & 4 &   1 & 2 & 3 & 4 &

Come on ba – by, light my fire.

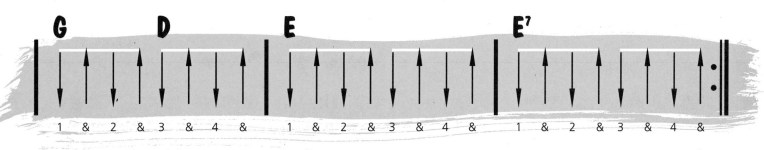

G   D   E   E⁷

1 & 2 & 3 & 4 &   1 & 2 & 3 & 4 &   1 & 2 & 3 & 4 &

Try to set the night on   fire.   2. The

READING MUSIC MADE EASY

THE STAVE

The music we play is written on five equally spaced lines called a **stave** or staff.

Staves are divided into **bars** (or measures) by the use of a vertical line.

Each bar has a fixed number of **beats** in it. A beat is the natural tapping rhythm of a song. Most songs have four beats in each bar, and we can tap our feet or count along with these songs.

| 1   2   3   4 | 1   2   3   4 | 1   2   3   4 |

Occasionally, there are three beats in each bar, and we count like this:

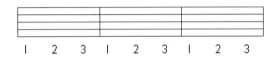

| 1   2   3 | 1   2   3 | 1   2   3 |

TIME SIGNATURES

At the beginning of every piece of music there are two numbers, written one above the other. This is called a **time signature**. The top number tells us how many beats are in a bar. The lower number tells us the value of these beats as expressed in the musical notation (this will be explained shortly).

The two most common time signatures in popular music are these:

4/4 is often shown as C, or **Common Time**.

Once given, the time signature is not repeated, unless the beat changes within a song. This happens only rarely in popular music.

CLEFS

The other symbol we find at the beginning of each stave is called the **treble clef**.

This fixes the pitch of the notes on the stave. The line that passes through the centre of the spiral, second up from the bottom, fixes the note G. We will look more at notes and pitch in a moment.

FORM NOTATION (REPEAT SIGNS)

In music there are various standard markings which can be used to abbreviate the layout. When we come to this sign:

it tells us to go back to where this sign appears:

(or sometimes when this does not appear, we return to the beginning) and **repeat** the section.

1ST & 2ND TIME BARS

Sometimes we repeat the whole section, but the ending of the 'second time through' can be different from the first time. Thus we have what are called **1st** and **2nd** time bars (or a 3rd and 4th for that matter.) Here is an example:

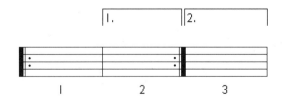

| 1 | 2 | 3 |

The first time through we play bars 1 and 2. The second time we play bars 1 and 3.

D.C. & D.S.

We often see the letters D.C. and D.S. at the end of a stave line. D.C. (from the Italian **da capo**) tells us to return to the beginning ('top'). D.S. (**dal segno**) means return to the sign (𝄋). After these letters we see the words al coda (**to the coda**) or al fine (to the finish). The coda is the end section of a song, usually short. Here is an example:

Here we plays bars 1-3. We are then directed back to bar 2, and continue to bar 3, when the sign (⊕) above the bar line tells us to jump to the coda at bar 4.

Here is another example:

Play bars 1-4. Then return to bar 1, and continue to bar 2, where the word Fine (or end) tells us to stop. Sometimes coupled with the word Fine we see the sign (⌢) over a chord or note. This means you pause on the beat marked, letting the final chord ring. This is a very common ending.

(𝄎) means that you should repeat the preceding bar.

is played

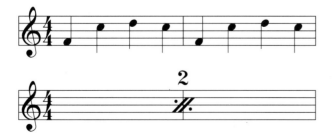

means that you should repeat the preceding two bars.

NOTE VALUES

Now we come to notes and their time values. The notes tell the player exactly what to play, how to play it, and when to play it.

Semibreve (or whole note):

Minim (or half note):

Crotchet (or quarter note):

Quaver (or eighth note):

Semiquaver (or sixteenth note):

The notes in each diagram all add up to 4 beats, the beat being 1 crotchet. Quavers and semiquavers are joined together with 'beams' to make the music tidier.

So in a piece of music in 4/4 time we count 4 beats to the bar, each beat being 1 crotchet:

A bar in 2/4 time will contain 2 crotchet beats per bar:

The same principle applies to 3/4 time:

DOTTED NOTES

Above, we see a minim with a **dot** after it.
The dot increases the time value of any note after which it is placed by half.

So, a **dotted minim**: 2 beats + 1 beat = 3 beats.

A **dotted crotchet**: $1 + \frac{1}{2} = 1\frac{1}{2}$ beats.

COUNTING

Many guitar accompaniments consist of strumming 8 quavers to each bar of 4/4 time. We still count 4 crotchets but to maintain an easy rhythm we count 1 & 2 & 3 & 4 &, each syllable being one quaver:

We can break this counting down further, so with semiquaver rhythms the count would be: 1e&a 2e&a 3e&a 4e&a, each syllable being one semi-quaver:

Sometimes we see dotted quavers and semiquavers joined together. Again we count four, but the rhythm does not flow smoothly as with 8 quavers to the bar, and we count like this:

RESTS

Just as notes tell us when to play, we have **rests** which tell us when not to play. There is a rest which corresponds in value to each type of note.

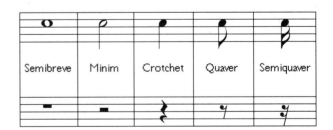

Semibreve	Minim	Crotchet	Quaver	Semiquaver

Similarly, dotted rests have the same time values as dotted notes.

A whole bar's rest is generally shown by a semibreve rest, whether or not the music is in 4/4 time.

PITCH

Here is the scale of **C major**.

A **tone** (T) is made up of **2 semitones** (S/T) and semitones correspond to the **frets** on your guitar, i.e. **C** to **D** is a tone or two frets, and **E** to **F** is a semitone or one fret.

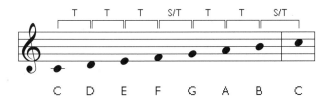

This is an octave and can be repeated up or down the stave.

LEGER LINES

The first C is below the stave and we see that a **leger** line runs through the note. This is an extension of the stave to accommodate the note. Here are more examples:

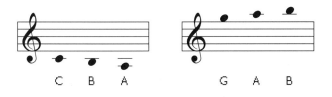

KEY SIGNATURE

At the beginning of each stave line we see, after the treble clef, the **key signature** of the music. This consists of sharps or flats or, in the case of C major or A minor none at all, and indicates that all notes against which they are set should be raised or lowered by a **semitone**.

Here, all **F**s are to be raised by a semitone in all octaves.

Here, all **B**s and **E**s are to be lowered by a semitone in all octaves:

ACCIDENTALS

It is necessary sometimes to insert **sharps** or **flats** that do not occur in the key signature. They are called **accidentals**. In this case we put the sign before the individual note, and its effect lasts for one bar only. The **natural** sign (♮) is also used to countermand a sharp or flat given in the key signature. Again its effect is for one bar only:

TIES

Finally we come to the curved line called a **tie**, which, in its various functions, will occur in this book.

It has the effect of joining together two notes. When you see two notes of the same pitch tied together you simply play the first one and let it ring on through the note to which it is tied.

These are the basic outlines of reading and understanding written music.

ADDITIONAL LYRICS

BLUE SUEDE SHOES

Verse 1
Well it's one for the money
Two for the show
Three to get ready, now go, cat, go...
But don't you step on my blue
suede shoes.
You can do anything but stay off
of my blue suede shoes.

Verse 2
Well you can knock me down
Step on my face
Slander my name all over the place
Do anything that you want to do
But ah-ah honey lay off of them
shoes...
And don't you step on my blue
suede shoes.
You can do anything but stay off
of my blue suede shoes.

Let's go cats!

Verse 3
You can burn my house, steal my car
Drink my liquor from an old fruit jar
Well do anything that you want to do
But ah-ah honey lay off of my shoes...
And don't you step on my blue
suede shoes.
You can do anything but stay off of
my blue suede shoes.

Verse 4
Well it's one for the money
Two for the show
Three to get ready, now go, go, go...
But don't you step on my blue
suede shoes.
You can do anything but stay off
of my blue suede shoes.

Coda
Well it's blue, blue, blue suede shoes
Blue, blue, blue suede shoes, yeah!
Blue, blue, blue suede shoes, baby!
Blue, blue, blue suede shoes
Well you can do anything but stay off
of my blue suede shoes.

DRIFTWOOD

Verse 1
Everything is open
Nothing is set in stone
Rivers turn to oceans
Oceans tide you home
Home is where the heart is
But your heart had to roam
Drifting over bridges
Never to return
Watching bridges burn.

Chorus
You're driftwood floating underwater
Breaking into pieces, pieces, pieces.
Just driftwood, hollow and of no use
Waterfalls will find you, bind you
Grind you.

Verse 2
Nobody is an island
Everyone has to go
Pillars turn to butter
Butter flying low
Low is where your heart is
But your heart has to grow
Drifting under bridges
Never with the flow.

Bridge
And you really didn't think it would
happen
But it really is the end of the line.

Chorus
So I'm sorry that you've turned
to driftwood
But you've been drifting for a long
long time.

Verse 3
Everywhere there's trouble
Nowhere's safe to go
Pushes turn to shovels
Shovelling the snow
Frozen you have chosen
The path you wish to go
Drifting now forever
And forever more
Until you reach your shore.

Chorus
You're driftwood floating underwater
Breaking into pieces, pieces, pieces.
Just driftwood, hollow and of no use
Waterfalls will find you, bind you
Grind you, and you...

Bridge
Really didn't think it would happen
But it really is the end of the line.

Chorus
So I'm sorry that you've turned
to driftwood
But you've been drifting for a long
long time
You've been drifting for a long, long
time
You've been drifting for a long, long
Drifting for a long, long time.

SAIL AWAY

Chorus
Sail away with me honey
I put my heart in your hands
Sail away with me honey now
Now, now.
Sail away with me
What will be will be
I wanna hold you now, now, now.

Verse 2
Crazy skies all wild above me now
Winter howling at my face
And everything I held so dear
Disappeared without a trace
Oh all the times I've tasted love
Never knew quite what I had
Little darling if you hear me now
Never needed you so bad
Spinning round inside my head.

Chorus

Verse 2
I've been talking drunken gibberish
Falling in and out of bars
Trying to get some explanation here
For the way some people are.
How did it ever come so far?

Repeat Chorus x 2

Verse 3
Sail away with me honey
I put my heart in your hands
You'll break me up if you put me
down, whoa———.
Sail away with me
What will be will be
I wanna hold you now, now, now.

WILD WOOD

Verse 1
High tide, mid-afternoon
People fly by in the traffic's boom
Knowing just where you're blowing
Getting to where
You should be going.

Verse 2
Don't let them get you down
Making you feel guilty about
Golden rain will bring you riches
All the good things you deserve now.

Verse 3
Climbing, forever trying
Find your way out
Of the wild wild wood.
Now there's no justice
You've only yourself
That you can trust in.

Verse 4
And I said, high tide, mid-afternoon
People fly by in the traffic's boom
Knowing just where you're blowing
Getting to where
You should be going.

Verse 5
Day by day, your world fades away
Waiting to feel all the dreams that say
Golden rain will bring you riches
All the good things you deserve now
And I say...

Verse 6
Climbing, forever trying
You're gonna find your way out
Of the wild, wild wood.
I said, you're gonna find your way out
Of the wild, wild wood.

ROLL WITH IT

Verse 1
You gotta roll with it
You gotta take your time
You gotta say what you say
Don't let anybody get in your way
'Cause it's all too much for me to take.

Verse 2
Don't ever stand aside
Don't ever be denied
You wanna be who you'd be
If you're coming with me.
I think I've got a feeling I've lost
inside
I think I'm gonna take me away
and hide
I'm thinking things that I just can't
abide.

Bridge
I know the roads down which your
life will drive
I find the key that lets you slip inside
Kiss the girl, she's not behind the door
But you know I think I recognise
your face
But I've never seen you before.

Repeat Verse 1

Instrumental

Repeat Bridge

Repeat Verse 1

Coda
Don't ever stand aside
Don't ever be denied
You wanna be who you'd be
If you're coming with me.

I think I've got a feeling I've lost
inside. *(repeat ad lib to fade)*

20TH CENTURY BOY

Verse 1
Friends say it's fine
Friends say it's good
Everybody says it's
Just like Robin Hood.
I move like a cat
Charge like a ram
Sting like a bee, babe!
I wanna be your man.

Chorus
But it's plain to see
You were meant for me, yeah
I'm your boy
Your Twentieth Century toy.

Verse 2
Friends say it's fine
Friends say it's good
Everybody says it's
Just like Robin Hood.
Fly like a plane, drive like a car
Bark like a hound, babe!
I wanna be your man.

Chorus 2
But it's plain to see
You were meant for me, yeah
I'm your toy
Your Twentieth Century boy.

Bridge
Twentieth century toy
I wanna be your boy.
Twentieth century boy
I wanna be your toy.
Twentieth century toy
I wanna be your boy.
Twentieth century boy
I wanna be your toy.

Repeat Verse 1

Repeat Chorus

Repeat Bridge

SHE LOVES YOU

Intro
She loves you, yeah, yeah, yeah
She loves you, yeah, yeah, yeah
She loves you, yeah, yeah, yeah, yeah.

Verse 1
You think you've lost your love
Well I saw her yesterday
It's you she's thinking of
And she told me what to say
She says she loves you
And you know that can't be bad
Yes, she loves you
And you know you should be glad.

Verse 2
She said you hurt her so
She almost lost her mind
But now she says she knows
You're not the hurting kind
She says she loves you
And you know that can't be bad
Yes, she loves you
And you know you should be glad.

Chorus
She loves you, yeah, yeah, yeah
She loves you, yeah, yeah, yeah
With a love like that
You know you should be glad.

Verse 3
You know it's up to you
I think it's only fair
Pride can hurt you too
Apologise to her
Because she loves you
And you know that can't be bad
Yes, she loves you
And you know you should be glad.

Chorus
She loves you, yeah, yeah, yeah
She loves you, yeah, yeah, yeah
With a love like that
You know you should be glad
With a love like that
You know you should be glad
With a love like that
You know you should be glad
Yeah, yeah, yeah
Yeah, yeah, yeah, yeah.

I SHOT THE SHERIFF

Chorus
I shot the sheriff
But I did not shoot the deputy.
I shot the sheriff
But I did not shoot the deputy.

Verse 1
All around in my hometown
They're trying to track me down
They say they want to bring me in
guilty
For the killing of a deputy
For the life of a deputy, but I say...

Chorus 1
I shot the sheriff
But I swear it was in self-defence.
I shot the sheriff
And they say it was a capital offence.

Verse 2
Sheriff John Brown always hated me
For what, I don't know
And every time that I plant a seed
He said kill it before it grows
He said kill it before it grows, I say...

Chorus 2
I shot the sheriff
But I swear it was in self-defence.
I shot the sheriff
But I swear it was in self-defence.

Verse 3
Freedom came my way one day
And I started out of town, yeah
All of a sudden I see Sheriff John
Brown
Aiming to shoot me down
So I shot, I shot him down, but I say...

Chorus 3
I shot the sheriff
But I did not shoot the deputy.
I shot the sheriff
But I did not shoot the deputy.

Verse 4
Reflexes got the better of me
And what is to be must be
Every day the bucket goes to the well
But one day the bottom will drop out
Yes, one day the bottom will drop out
But I say...

Chorus 4
I shot the sheriff
But I did not shoot the deputy.
I shot the sheriff
But I did not shoot no deputy.

SUNNY AFTERNOON

Verse 1
The tax man's taken all my dough
And left me in my stately home
Lazing on a sunny afternoon
And I can't sail my yacht
He's taken everything I've got
All I've got's this sunny afternoon.

Chorus
Save me, save me, save me from
this squeeze
I got a big fat mama trying to
break me.
And I love to live so pleasantly
Live this life of luxury
Lazing on a sunny afternoon.
In the summertime
In the summertime
In the summertime.

Verse 2
My girlfriend's run off with my car
And gone back to her ma and pa
Telling tales of drunkenness and
cruelty.
Now I'm sitting here
Sipping at my ice cold beer
Lazing on a sunny afternoon.

Chorus 2
Help me, help me, help me sail away
Well give me two good reasons
Why I oughta stay.
'Cause I love to live so pleasantly
Live this life of luxury
Lazing on a sunny afternoon.
In the summertime
In the summertime
In the summertime.

Chorus 3
Save me, save me, save me from
this squeeze
I got a big fat mama trying to
break me.
And I love to live so pleasantly
Live this life of luxury
Lazing on a sunny afternoon.
In the summertime
In the summertime
In the summertime
In the summertime
In the summertime.

THERE SHE GOES

Verse 1
There she goes
There she goes again
Racing through my brain
And I just can't contain
This feeling that remains.

Verse 2
There she goes
There she goes again
Pulsing through my vein
And I just can't contain
This feeling that remains.

Bridge
There she goes
There she goes again
She calls my name, pulls my train
No-one else could heal my pain.
But I just can't contain
This feeling that remains.

Verse 3
There she goes
There she goes again
Chasing down my lanes
And I just can't contain
This feeling that remains.

Coda
There she goes
There she goes
There she goes.

HEY JOE

Verse 1

Hey Joe, where you goin' with that
gun in your hand?
Hey Joe, I said where you goin' with
that gun in your hand?
I'm going out to shoot my old lady
You know I caught her messin' round
with another man.
I'm going down to shoot my old lady
You know I caught her messin' round
with another man.
(And that ain't too cool.)

Verse 2

Hey Joe, I heard you shot your woman
down, you shot her down now.
Hey Joe, I heard you shot your lady
down, shot her down to the ground.
Yes, I did, I shot her
You know I caught her messin' round,
messin' round town.
I did, I shot her, you know I caught my
old lady messin' around town.
And I gave her the gun, I shot her!

Guitar solo

Verse 3

Hey Joe, where you gonna run to
now?
Hey Joe, where you gonna run to now
(where you gonna go)?
Well, I'm going way down south
Way down to Mexico Way, alright!
Well, I'm going way down south
Way down where I can be free
Ain't no hang man gonna
He ain't gonna put a rope around me.
(You'd better believe, right now.)
Hey Joe, you'd better run now.

ALL RIGHT NOW

Verse 1

There she stood, in the street
Smiling from her head to her feet.
I said 'Hey, what is this?'
Now baby maybe
Maybe she's in need of a kiss?
I said 'Hey, what's your name baby?
Maybe we can see things the same'.
Now don't you wait, or hesitate
Let's move before they raise the
parking rate. Ow!

Chorus

All right now, baby it's all right now.
All right now, baby it's all right now.

Verse 2

I took her home to my place
Watching every move on her face.
She said 'Look, what's your game?
Are you tryin' to put me in shame?'
I said 'Slow! Don't go so fast
Don't you think that love can last?'
She said 'Love? Lord above!
Now you're tryin' to trick me in love.'

Chorus

All right now, baby it's all right now.
All right now, baby it's all right now.

Instrumental

Repeat Verse 2

Repeat Chorus to fade

NIGHTS IN WHITE SATIN

Verse 1

Nights in white satin
Never reaching the end
Letters I've written
Never meaning to send.
Beauty I'd always missed
With these eyes before
Just what the truth is
I can't say anymore.

Chorus

'Cause I love you
Yes I love you
Oh, how I love you.

Verse 2

Gazing at people
Some hand in hand
Just what I'm doing
They can't understand.
Some try to tell me
Thoughts they cannot defend
Just what you want to be
You'll be in the end.

Chorus

And I love you
Yes I love you
Oh, how I love you.

Repeat Verse 1

Repeat Chorus x 2

WHILE MY GUITAR GENTLY WEEPS

Verse 1
I look at you all, see the love there
that's sleeping
While my guitar gently weeps.
I look at the floor and I see it needs
sweeping
Still my guitar gently weeps.

Bridge 1
I don't know why nobody told you
How to unfold your love
I don't know how someone
controlled you
They bought and sold you.

Verse 2
I look at the world and I notice it's
turning
While my guitar gently weeps.
With every mistake we must surely
be learning
Still my guitar gently weeps.

Guitar solo

Bridge 2
I don't know how, you were diverted
You were perverted too.
I don't know how you were inverted
No one alerted you.

Verse 3
I look at you all, see the love there
that's sleeping
While my guitar gently weeps.
I look at you all...
Still my guitar gently weeps.

PINBALL WIZARD

Verse 1
Ever since I was a young boy
I played the silver ball
From Soho down to Brighton
I must have played 'em all.
But I ain't seen nothin' like him
In any amusement hall
That deaf, dumb, and blind kid
Sure plays a mean pinball.

Verse 1
He stands like a statue
Becomes part of the machine
Feelin' all the bumpers
Always playin' clean.
Plays by intuitition
The digit counters fall
That deaf, dumb and blind kid
Sure plays a mean pinball.

Chorus
He's a pinball wizard
There has to be a twist
A pinball wizard
Got such a supple wrist.
How do you think he does it?
(I don't know)
What makes him so good?

Verse 3
Ain't got no distractions
Can't hear no buzzes and bells
Don't see no lights a-flashin'
Plays by sense of smell.
Always gets a replay
Never see him fall
That deaf, dumb and blind kid
Sure plays a mean pinball.

Bridge
I thought I was the body table king
But I just handed my pinball crown
to him.

Instrumental

Verse 4
He's been on my fav'rite table
He can beat my best
His disciples lead him in
And he just does the rest.
He's got crazy flippin' fingers
Never see him fall
That deaf, dumb and blind kid
Sure plays a mean pinball.

LIGHT MY FIRE

Verse 1
You know that it would be untrue
You know that I would be a liar
If I was to say to you
Girl, we couldn't get much higher.

Chorus
Come on baby, light my fire
Come on baby, light my fire
Try to set the night on fire.

Verse 2
The time to hesitate is through
No time to wallow in the myre
Try now, we can only lose
And our love become a funeral pyre.

Chorus
Come on baby, light my fire
Come on baby, light my fire
Try to set the night on fire.

Instrumental

Repeat Verse 2

Repeat Chorus

Repeat Verse 1

Repeat Chorus

The Complete Rock & Pop Guitar Player
Part 3

INTRODUCTION

Welcome to *The Complete Rock & Pop Guitar Player Part 3*. If you're reading this then you've completed Parts 1 and 2 of the course, and you're well on your way to becoming an accomplished guitarist.

You are now familiar with playing from strumming patterns, chord boxes and lyrics, and have also started to read guitar tablature. **Part 3** will feature more tab, new chords and more well-known hit songs, as well as a section on guitar effects which explains the many sounds available to an electric guitarist.

The songs are graded as before, introducing new chords, strumming patterns or other techniques as you go along, and full lyrics are included at the back of the book.

As with the previous parts of this course, **Part 3** is ideal for learning with or without a teacher, and the musical examples are demonstrated on the CD for Part 3 in high-quality 'soundalike' recordings.

ELECTRONIC EFFECTS FOR GUITAR

One of the great things about amplification is that you can alter the sound of your guitar *en route* to the amplifier with the use of electronic sound effects. To do this you will need one extra lead per effect.

If you have more than one effect it is best for your own mobility to have a long lead between the guitar and the first effect, then very short leads between the effects themselves to keep down the level of unwanted electrical interference. Finally, a long lead between the last effect and the amplifier will give you greater flexibility in positioning yourself for easy access to the pedals.

VOLUME PEDALS

These provide foot controlled volume level changes. They are very useful as they leave your hands free to concentrate on playing. As this was one of the first 'gimmicks' to become available to the electric guitar player it is probably for this reason that effects boxes are known as pedals.

'WAH-WAH' PEDALS

Trumpet players use a mute to get a wah-wah sound, guitarists use a pedal. Most wah-wahs have a filter which shifts the emphasis of the sound from bass to treble. With the heel down the lower frequencies are boosted, with the toe down the higher frequencies are boosted.

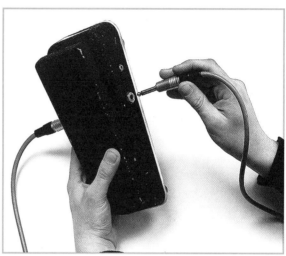

THE AUTO-WAH OR ENVELOPE FILTER

This produces sounds which are similar to a wah-wah pedal. However, rather than having the filter responding to the position of the foot, it responds to the dynamics of your playing. In other words, hitting the strings harder increases treble emphasis and playing lightly produces more bass response.

GRAPHIC EQUALIZER

This device is a sophisticated form of tone control. It allows you to boost or cut many more frequencies than the bass/treble controls on your guitar or amplifier. Using a graphic equalizer opens the door to a completely new spectrum of sounds and for that reason is a very useful effect.

FUZZ AND OVERDRIVE PEDALS AND EFFECTS

Both these types of pedals produce basically the same effect. They overload (overdrive) a section of the circuit of the pedal or the amplifier pre-amp. This gives the notes or chords a much fuller sound and produces much more sustain. The pedals also tend to boost the treble (or top) frequencies of the sound, so it is better to buy one which incorporates a tone control to counteract this. You will find that changing the volume setting on your guitar will alter the intensity of the fuzz.

THE COMPRESSOR

Here is a graph of a guitar string being plucked:

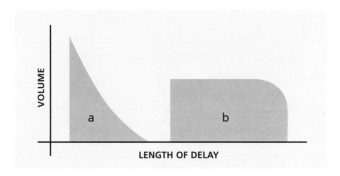

LENGTH OF DELAY

The volume refers to the loudness of the note and the time of decay to the length of time it lasts. Example (a) shows a natural sound and example (b) a compressed one. You will see that the natural sound starts loudly and dies away, whereas the compressed one starts at half the volume but stays there for much longer before quickly dying away. This is what a compressor does. It gives sustain, and is very useful for providing the 'pedal steel' type sound which is synonymous with country music.

CHORUS PEDAL

One of the most useful effects for a beginner is the chorus pedal which gives a pleasant jangly sound to your chords. The unit achieves this effect by constantly altering the frequency (in cycles) of a given note (or notes) to just above, and just below, its original pitch.

ECHO UNITS AND REVERB

Along with distortion, reverb is possibly the most useful effect to have in your amplifier. Reverb makes your guitar sound as though it is in a large room or hall. This is great for getting a fuller sound at lower volumes and goes very well with chorus.

Echo units duplicate your notes at a variety of times after the note you have played. Short echoes will thicken your sound; longer echoes can work well on lead solos. The trick is to adjust the time delay, the number of repeats and the volume of the echo compared to the original note, for the best musical effect.

ANALOGUE DELAY

Analogue delay uses a technique generally referred to as the 'bucket brigade device' which simply passes the sound through a series of stages (or buckets) until it emerges from the end of the delay line later (in time) than the original sound which is allowed to pass through the unit unaffected. You can usually mix the volume of the affected and unaffected signal to attain the amount of echo you require.

DIGITAL DELAY

Digital delay is generally accepted as offering the highest fidelity and is therefore more expensive. A typical unit works by sampling the sound and immediately converting it from an audio signal into a digital code, which represents the voltage value. This code word then passes down a series of stages called shift registers and when it emerges it will have been 'delayed' before being decoded back into an audio signal at its original voltage level.

The advantage of this technique is that the decoder at the end of the line recognises only the code word and not the noise which may have accumulated to distort it. So when it changes the code back into audio signal voltage it will sound a great deal closer to the original sound than is possible with other types of units.

MULTI-EFFECTS UNITS

The other type of device you may wish to consider is a multi-effect unit, for example, the Line6 POD. This combines many of the effects previously mentioned into one small compact unit. Using a foot pedal in conjunction allows you to switch easily and quickly between effects, for instance when you're playing solos. It all depends on your budget and the range of effects you're looking for.

MRS ROBINSON
Words & Music by Paul Simon

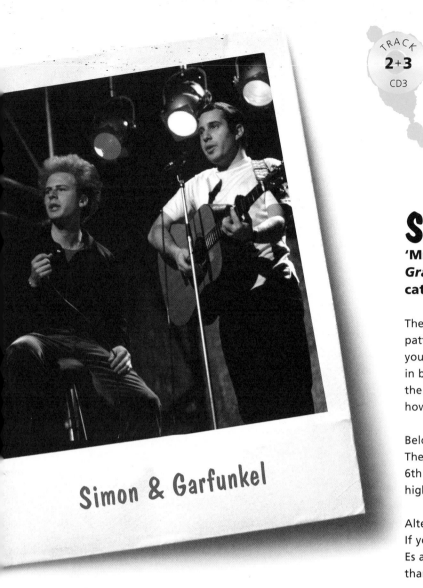

Simon & Garfunkel

Simon & Garfunkel were one of the most popular male duos of the 1960s. 'Mrs Robinson', taken from the film *The Graduate*, charted in 1968 and 1969 with its catchy chorus and acoustic-driven verse.

There are no new chords for this song. For the strumming pattern you need to play the root note of the chord with your thumb, and then strum the chord. Watch out for the ties in bars 5 and 13. Play the upstrum, then count '1' and play on the '&'. Listen to the CD for Part 3 for a demonstration of how this should sound.

Below is the guitar riff that links the chorus to the verse. There are two ways of playing this. You can play the open 6th string with your thumb, and use your fingers to play the higher notes.

Alternatively, you can use a pick to play the 6th string notes. If you find the timing tricky remember that all the 6th string Es are on the beat, so fit the higher notes to them rather than the other way round.

MAIN GUITAR RIFF

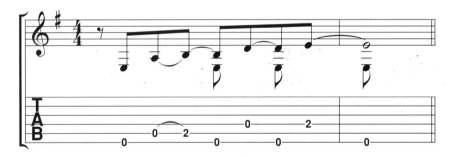

CAPO 3RD FRET
4 BAR 'FADE IN' INTRO

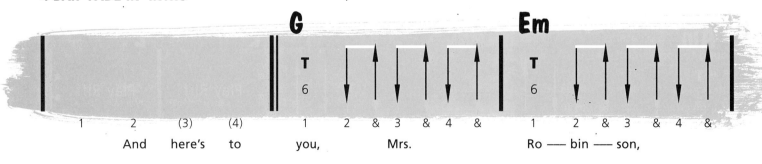

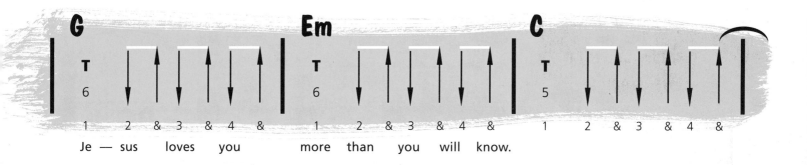

G — **Em** — **C**

Je — sus loves you more than you will know.

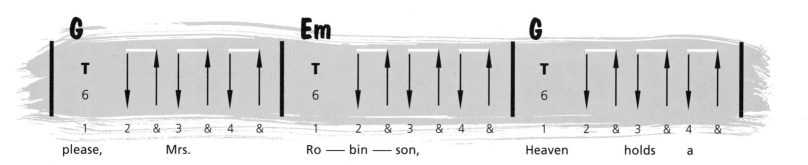

C — **D⁷** — **D⁷**

Wo, wo, wo God bless you

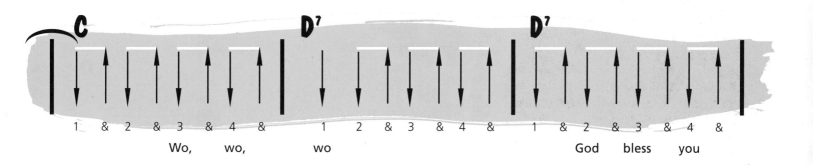

G — **Em** — **G**

please, Mrs. Ro — bin — son, Heaven holds a

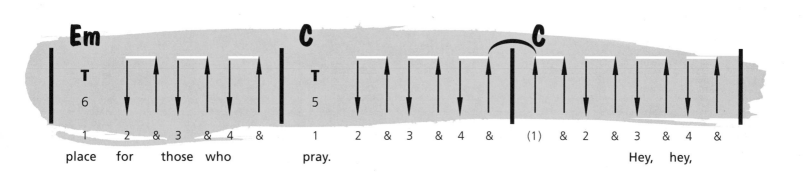

Em — **C** — **C**

place for those who pray. Hey, hey,

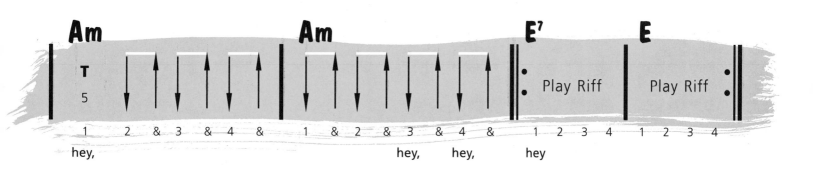

Am — **Am** — **E⁷** — **E**

hey, hey, hey, hey

Play Riff   Play Riff

YELLOW

Words & Music by
Guy Berryman, Jon Buckland,
Will Champion & Chris Martin

Bsus4

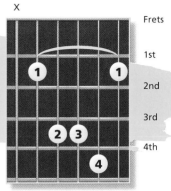

F♯6 Chord

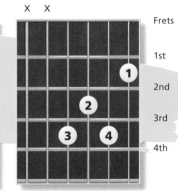

Emaj7

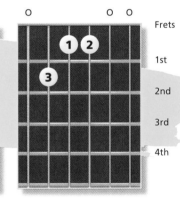

For this recent hit by Coldplay we need to learn three new chords: **Bsus4**, **F♯6** and **Emaj7**.

If you find the barre version of **Bsus4** too hard, just use the four-string **B** chord and add the little finger on the 5th fret of the 2nd string. Another way to cheat at this (which happens to fit this song) is to hold the four-string **B** chord and lift your first finger off the top string. Strictly speaking this isn't a **sus4** but it is close enough to suit '**Yellow**'.

This **F♯6** is an abbreviated version of the full **F♯6** chord. Think of it as a half-barre **F** moved to the second fret with the 4th finger adding an extra note. You should find the **Emaj7** easy. This shape is easier to play than some of the more common **Emaj7** shapes and fits the chorus.

The **G♯m** on the chorus is simply an **F♯m** shape (which you learned in '**Dance Away**' in Part 1) moved up two frets.

The strumming on '**Yellow**' is steady 8ths throughout.

2 BAR 'FADE IN' INTRO
VERSE

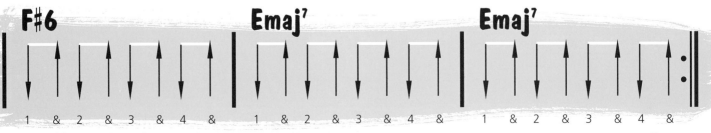

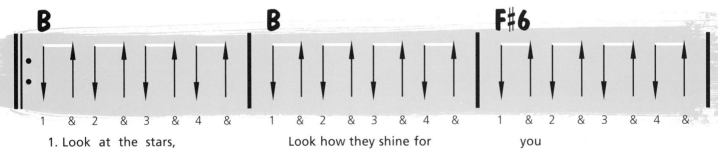

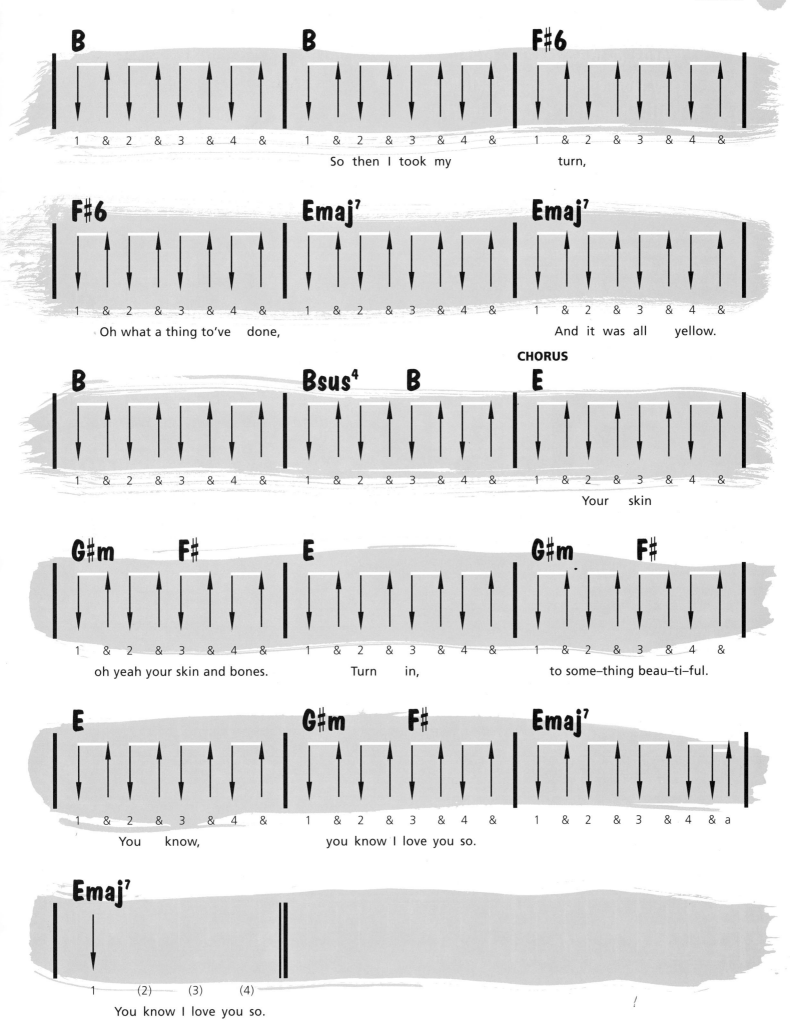

B

1 & 2 & 3 & 4 &

B

1 & 2 & 3 & 4 &
So then I took my

F#6

1 & 2 & 3 & 4 &
turn,

F#6

1 & 2 & 3 & 4 &
Oh what a thing to've done,

Emaj⁷

1 & 2 & 3 & 4 &

Emaj⁷

1 & 2 & 3 & 4 &
And it was all yellow.

B

1 & 2 & 3 & 4 &

Bsus⁴ **B**

1 & 2 & 3 & 4 &

CHORUS
E

1 & 2 & 3 & 4 &
Your skin

G#m **F#**

1 & 2 & 3 & 4 &
oh yeah your skin and bones.

E

1 & 2 & 3 & 4 &
Turn in,

G#m **F#**

1 & 2 & 3 & 4 &
to some–thing beau–ti–ful.

E

1 & 2 & 3 & 4 &
You know,

G#m **F#**

1 & 2 & 3 & 4 &
you know I love you so.

Emaj⁷

1 & 2 & 3 & 4 & a

Emaj⁷

1 (2) (3) (4)
You know I love you so.

A WHITER SHADE OF PALE
Words by Keith Reid, Music by Gary Brooker

Procol Harum

This beautiful ballad by Procol Harum is a classic 1960s pop song that went to No.1 around the world.

This song uses three inversions: **G/B**, **G/D** and **C/E**. This is because the song's progression is marked by a descending bass line; the inversions help to reproduce it. With the strum pattern you are directed to pick the bass note on its own before you hit the chord.

Dm/C Chord

G/D Chord

Here's the intro melody. You can either count 8 bars from the beginning and then start strumming, or you could try playing this first, and then move on to the strumming.

INTRO

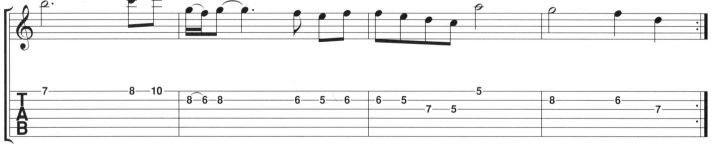

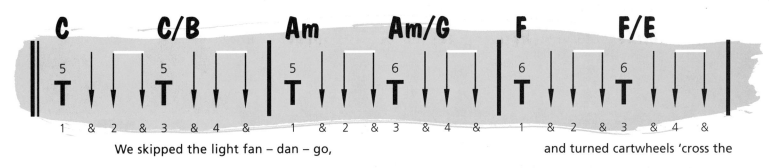

We skipped the light fan – dan – go,   and turned cartwheels 'cross the

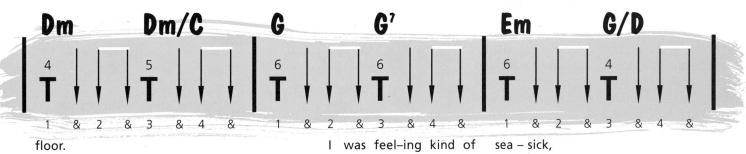

floor.   I was feel–ing kind of   sea – sick,

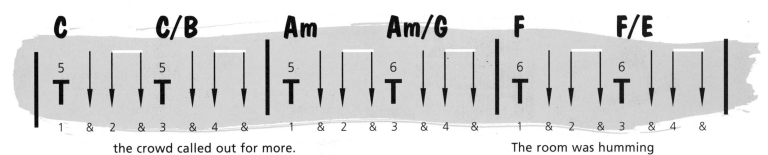

the crowd called out for more.   The room was humming

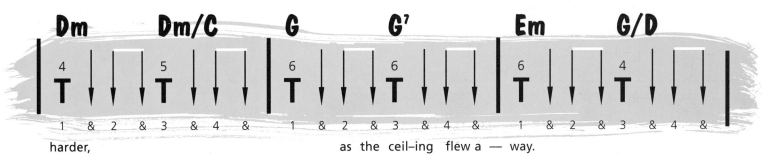

harder,   as the ceil–ing flew a — way.

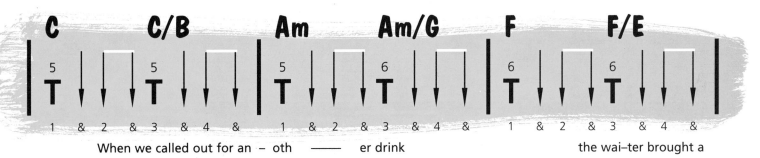

When we called out for an – oth —— er drink   the wai–ter brought a

CHORUS

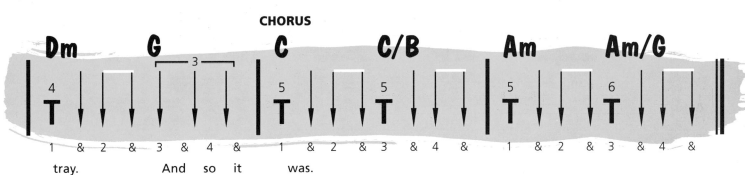

tray.   And so it   was.

TRACK
8+9
CD3

LAYLA
Words & Music by Eric Clapton & Jim Gordon

Eric Clapton

'Layla' comes from Eric Clapton's 1970 album **Layla and Other Assorted Love Songs,** under the name of Derek and the Dominoes.

A chart hit several times, it remains one of rock's most dynamic love songs. You already know all the chord shapes for this song. The **G#m7** and **C#m7** chords use the same shapes as **F#m7** and **Bm7**, both moved up two frets. The **B♭** can be played by taking a **B** chord and moving it down one fret. The main challenge here is the strumming.

In the verse '**Layla**' makes partial use of a 16th strum, so keep your strumming hand relaxed. The chorus rhythm is less of a rock pattern, and more of a soul influence.

When you've got used to the chords you can try the famous intro riff. The hammer-ons and pull-offs in the first bar are optional, but help you to play faster.

GUITAR RIFF

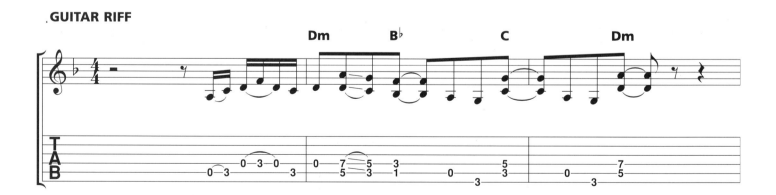

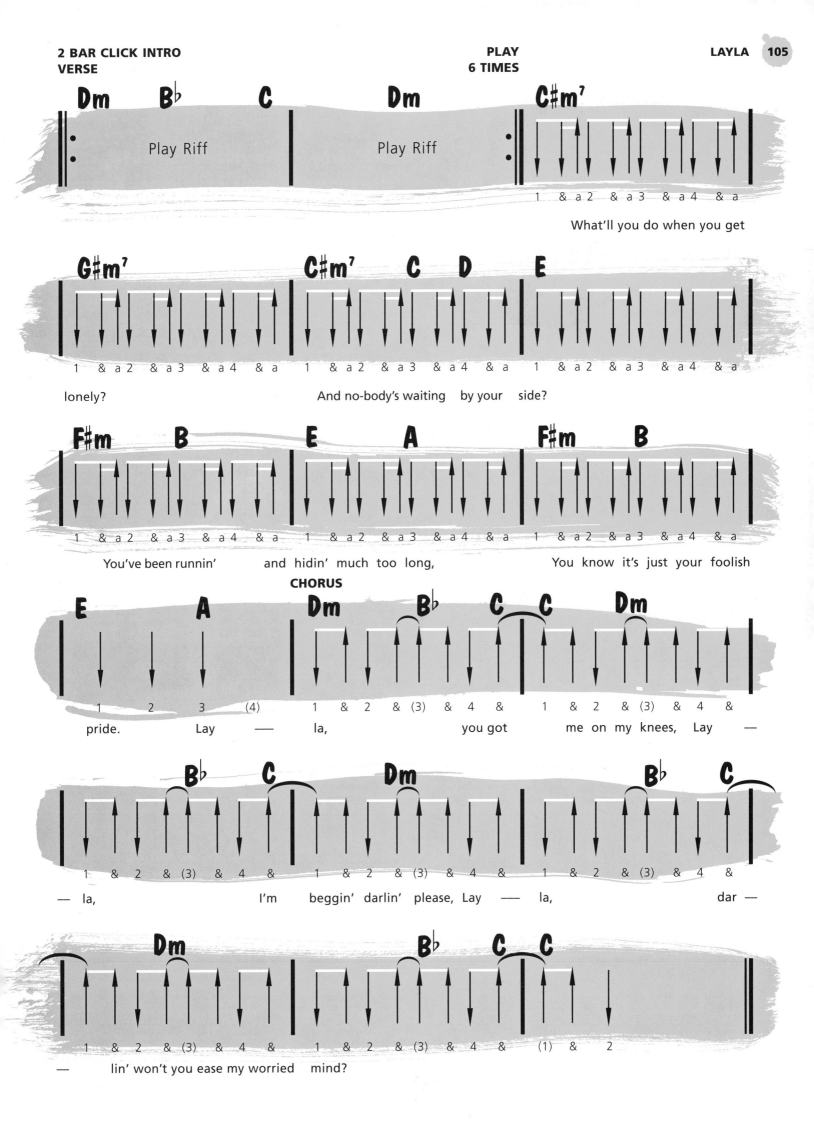

Bryan Adams

(EVERYTHING I DO) I DO IT FOR YOU

Words by Bryan Adams & Robert John Lange, Music by Michael Kamen

From the Kevin Costner film *Robin Hood*, 'Everything I Do' proved to be one of the biggest hits of the 1990s.

There are no new chords here, so you can concentrate on the alternating picking and strumming patterns. For the verse chords, you can get away with holding down partial shapes as you should only strum the top 3 strings (in between picking the D string).

For the **A/D**, after playing the **D** chord, move your second finger from the E string to the B string, and for the **G/D** shape, you only need to hold down the third finger on the E string at the 3rd fret.

2 BAR CLICK + 4 BAR PIANO INTRO
VERSE (First time around, strum 1st beat of each bar only for bars 1-8)

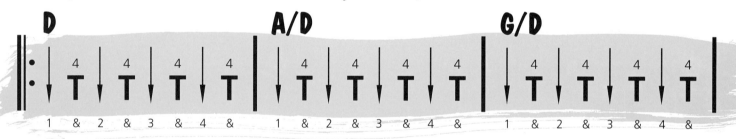

1.   Look into my eyes,   you will see,   what   you mean   to
2.   Look into your heart,   you will find,   there's   no – thing   left   to

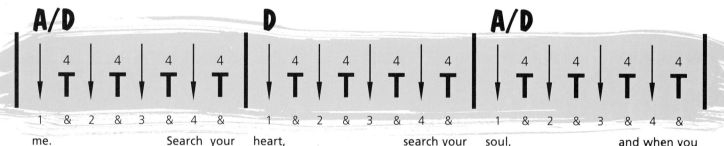

me.   Search your   heart,   search your   soul,   and when you
hide.   Take me as I   am,   take my   life,   I would

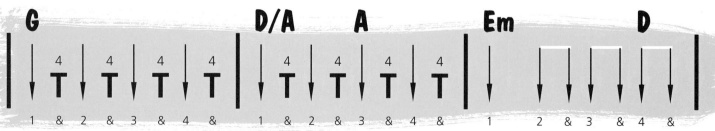

find   me   there   you'll   search   no more.   Don't   tell   me   it's not worth try–ing
give   it   all,   I would   sac —   ri – fice.   Don't   tell   me   it's not worth fight–ing

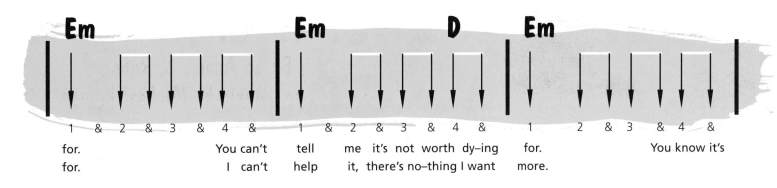

Em | **Em** | **D** | **Em**

1 & 2 & 3 & 4 & | 1 & 2 & 3 & 4 & | 1 2 & 3 & 4 &

for. You can't tell me it's not worth dy–ing for. You know it's
for. I can't help it, there's no–thing I want more.

CHORUS

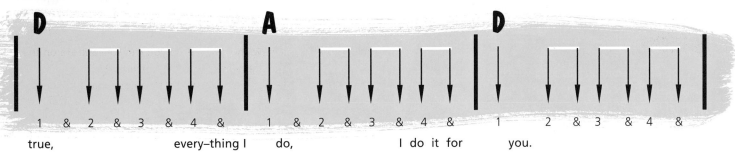

D | **A** | **D**

1 & 2 & 3 & 4 & | 1 & 2 & 3 & 4 & | 1 2 & 3 & 4 &

true, every–thing I do, I do it for you.

BRIDGE

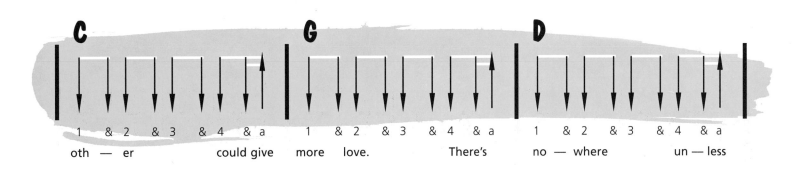

D | **C** | **F**

1 & 2 & 3 & 4 & | 1 & 2 & 3 & 4 & a | 1 & 2 & 3 & 4 & a

There's no love like your love, and no

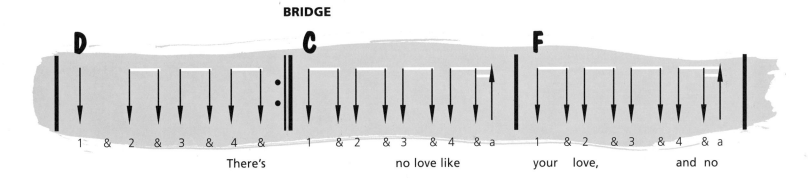

C | **G** | **D**

1 & 2 & 3 & 4 & a | 1 & 2 & 3 & 4 & a | 1 & 2 & 3 & 4 & a

oth — er could give more love. There's no — where un — less

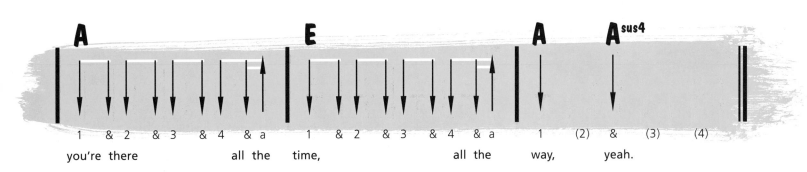

A | **E** | **A** **A**sus4

1 & 2 & 3 & 4 & a | 1 & 2 & 3 & 4 & a | 1 (2) & (3) (4)

you're there all the time, all the way, yeah.

MESSAGE IN A BOTTLE
Words & Music by Sting

Well, it's now time for a challenge. There are no new chords in 'Message In A Bottle' (a No.1 for The Police in 1979) but the guitar riff itself will be an excellent stretching exercise.

Think of it as four three-note figures. Drop your thumb lower behind the neck to open out your hand. Take the first note with your 1st finger, the second with your 2nd finger and the third with your 4th finger. This riff is played throughout the verse.

If you are strumming this song watch out for the damping in the chorus. You need to mute the strings a little and emphasise the lower notes of each chord until you get to **C#m7**. At the end of the chorus, get ready for the riff again.

The Police

RIFF

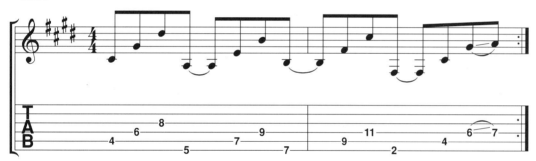

2 BAR CLICK + 4 BAR INTRO (RIFF)
VERSE & RIFF

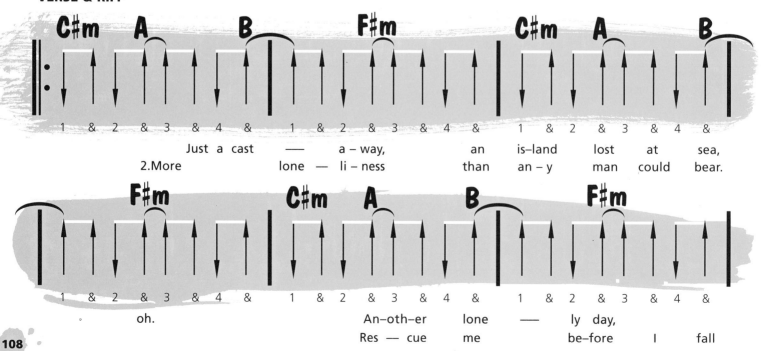

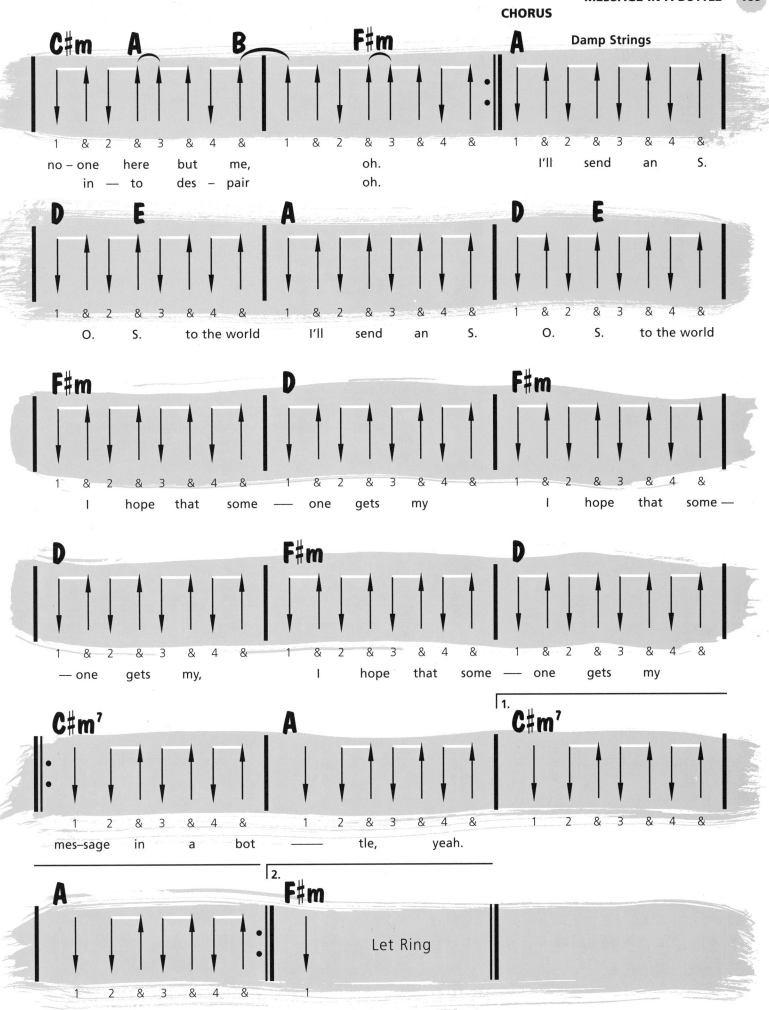

Dire Straits

SULTANS OF SWING
Words & Music by Mark Knopfler

This early hit for Dire Straits is justly renowned for its intricate lead guitar fills and solos.

To play the rhythm part you need to use that percussive 'click' technique used before. Here I will mention another way of doing it. Wherever you see a little cross ('**x**') on a beat let the side of your strumming hand hit the strings a fraction of a second before the pick does. If you make your hand strike the strings inward toward the guitar an extra percussive noise is made by the strings themselves hitting the metal frets. So the first verse bar is strummed:
1 'click' & 3 & 'click' &.

Here in TAB is the famous chorus **riff**. Notice the chords only have three notes. Mark Knopfler plays with his fingers rather than a pick, so it is natural to play triads by striking them with the thumb and first and second fingers.

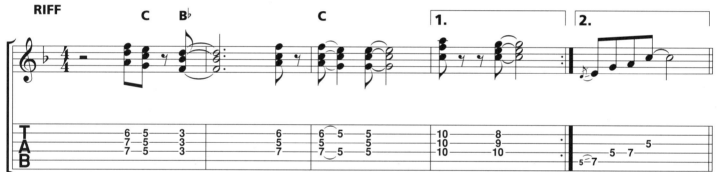

2 BAR CLICK + 8 BAR INTRO (DM CHORD)
VERSE

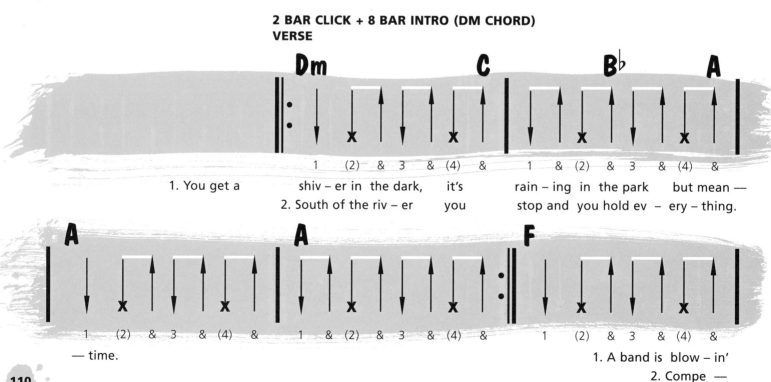

1. You get a shiv – er in the dark, it's rain – ing in the park but mean —
2. South of the riv – er you stop and you hold ev – ery – thing.

— time.

1. A band is blow – in'
2. Compe —

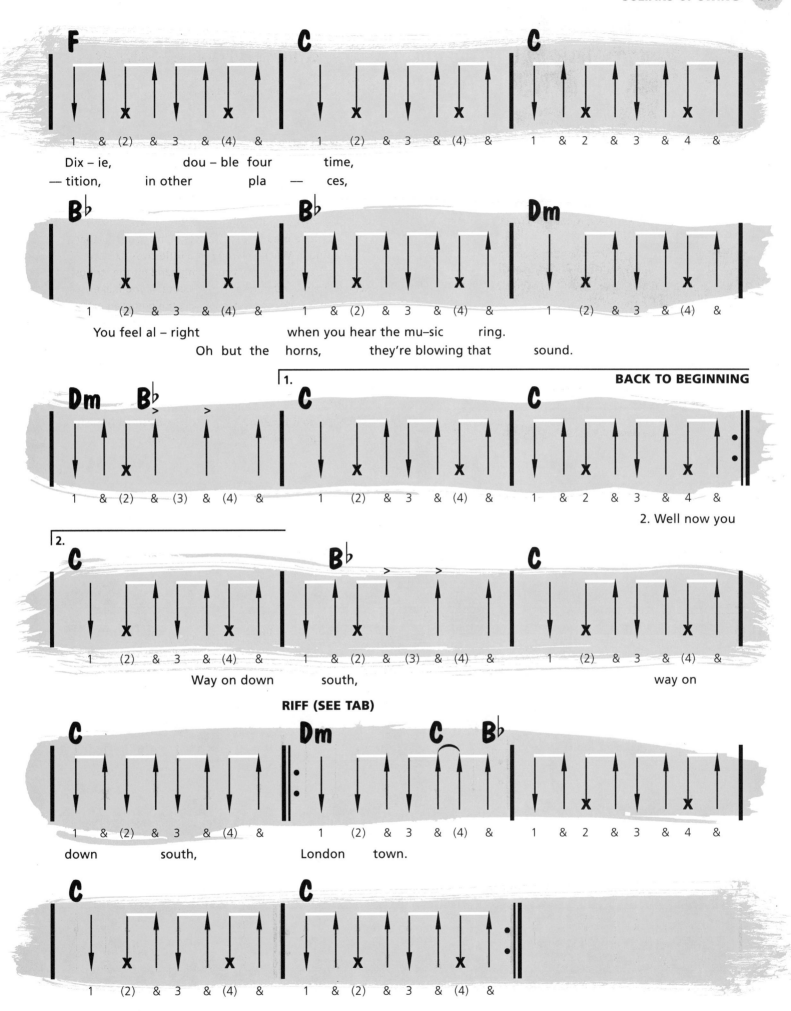

MULDER AND SCULLY

Words & Music by Cerys Matthews, Mark Roberts, Aled Richards, Paul Jones & Owen Powell

To play the opening track of Catatonia's *International Velvet* album you will need several new chord shapes: Amaj7, A6, Dmaj7, C#7 and an alternative shape for A major, A*.

Most of the strumming for this song is easy. The only tricky bit is the first bar with its quick change of chords and the 16th notes. Listen carefully to the CD to help you get a feel for the timing.

A* Chord

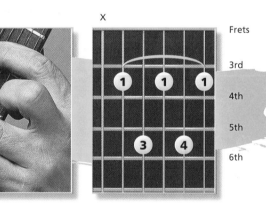

Amaj7 Chord

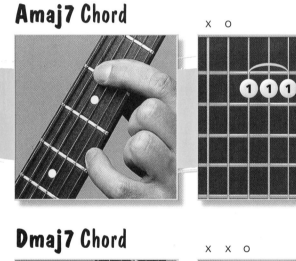

A6 Chord

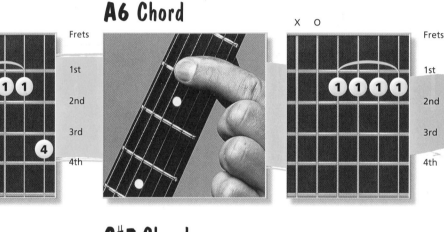

Dmaj7 Chord

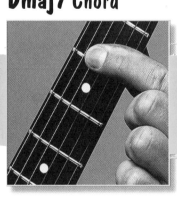

C#7 Chord

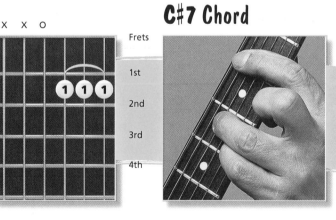

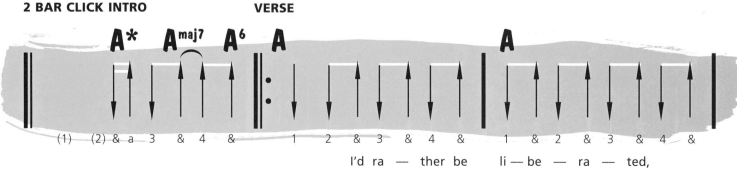

2 BAR CLICK INTRO   **VERSE**

A*   A^maj7   A^6   A   A

(1) (2) & a 3 & 4 &   1   2   & 3 & 4 &   1 & 2 & 3 & 4 &

I'd ra — ther be   li — be — ra — ted,
I'd ra — ther stay   bold   and lone — ly,

112

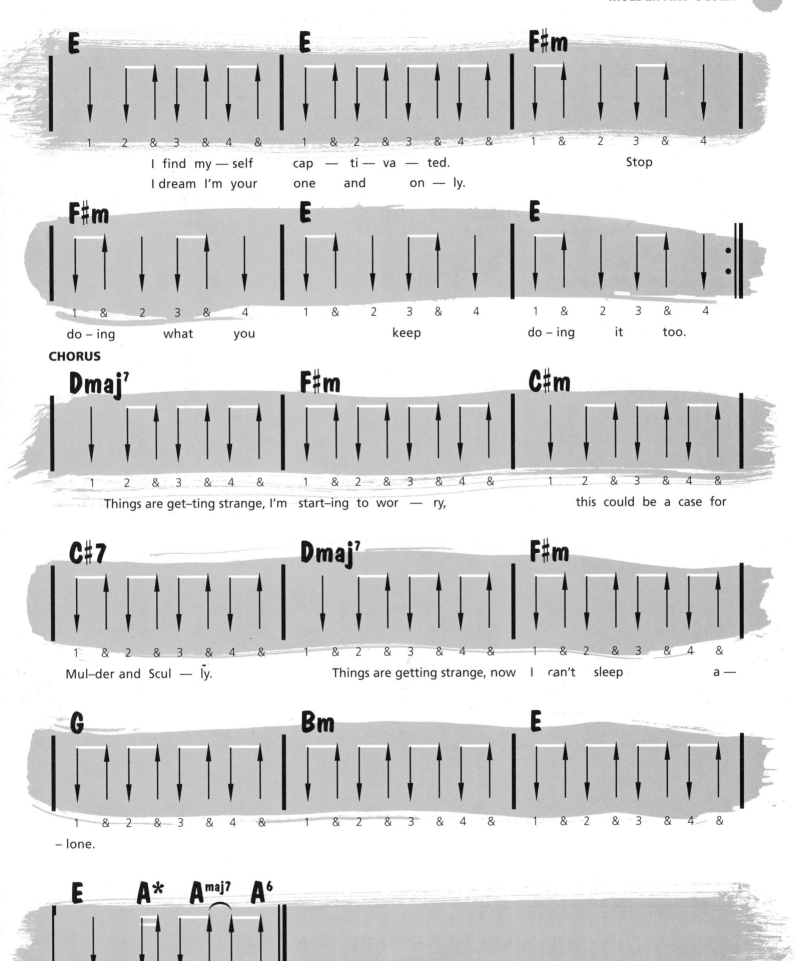

GOODBYE YELLOW BRICK ROAD
Words & Music by Elton John & Bernie Taupin

G#7 Chord

The title track of Elton John's 1973 double album is a slow tempo song with plenty of chord changes. However, all but one of the chords you already know. The new chord is G#7, shown here.

This shape is derived from the full barre major chord **F**, with the little finger lifted off to create the seventh.

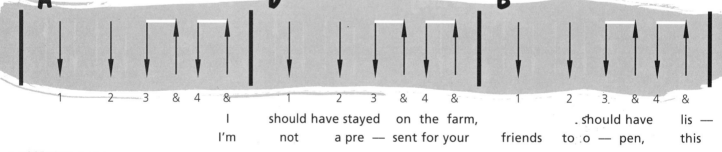

2 BAR CLICK INTRO + 4 BAR PIANO INTRO

CAPO 1ST FRET

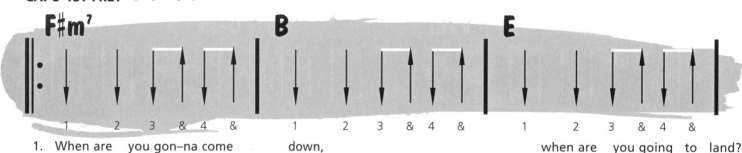

F#m⁷   **B**   **E**

1   2   3 & 4 &   1   2   3 & 4 &   1   2   3 & 4 &

1. When are   you gon–na come   down,   when are   you going   to   land?
(2.) know you can't hold   me for – ev ——   er,   I   didn't   sign up   with you.

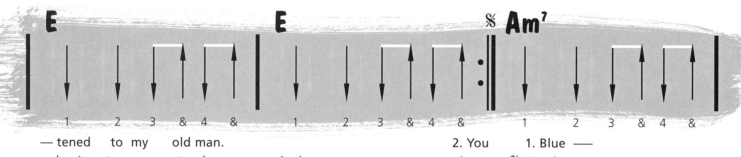

A   **D**   **B**

1   2   3 & 4 &   1   2   3 & 4 &   1   2   3 & 4 &

      I   should have stayed   on   the   farm,   should have   lis —
      I'm   not   a pre — sent for your   friends   to o — pen,   this

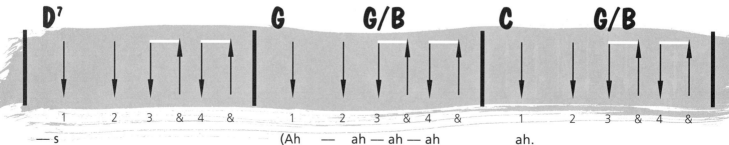

E   **E**   %. **Am⁷**

1   2   3 & 4 &   1   2   3 & 4 &   1   2   3 & 4 &

— tened   to my   old man.   2. You   1. Blue ——
boy's   too young   to   be   singing   the   %. Road

D⁷   **G**   **G/B**   **C**   **G/B**

1   2   3 & 4 &   1   2   3 & 4 &   1   2   3 & 4 &

— s   (Ah —   ah — ah — ah   ah.

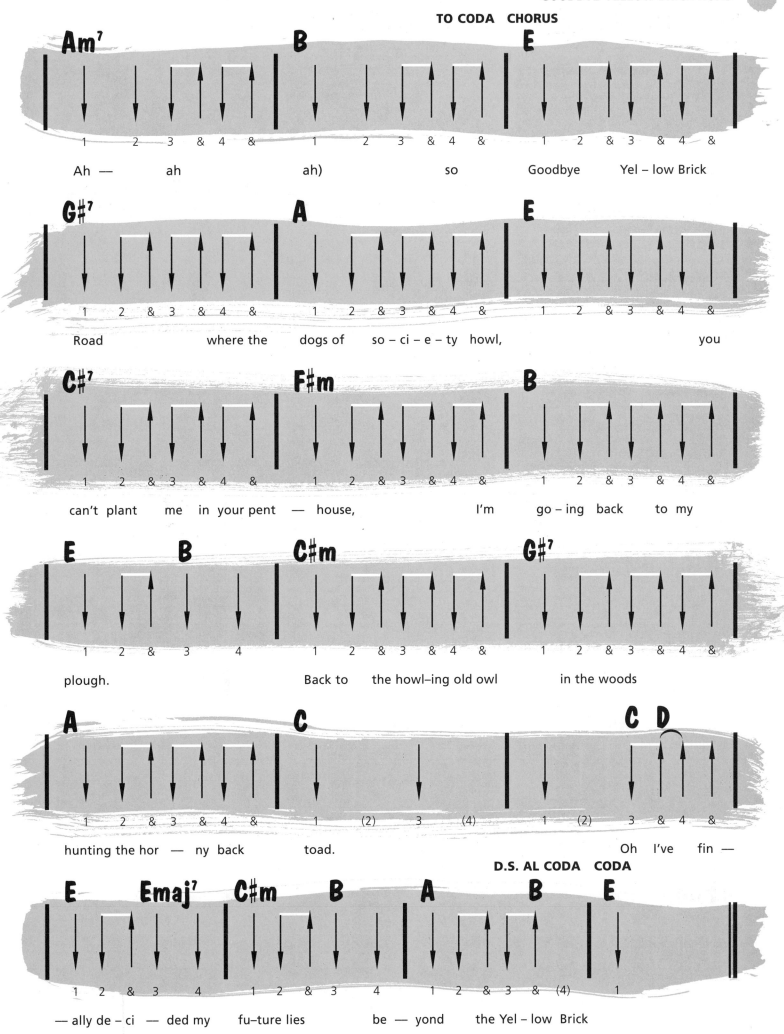

KNOWING ME, KNOWING YOU
Words & Music by Benny Andersson, Björn Ulvaeus & Stig Anderson

You will notice a Bsus2 in the music for this Abba song. It occurs just before the chorus on the word 'Goodbye'.

This chord is based on the **Asus2** open shape, where you simply hold down **A** and take your finger off the **B** string. Here it is turned into a movable barre chord. The **sus2** chord is not as tense as the **sus4**.

Note that the second to last bar is in 2/4 time, which means that you count 1&2& only, before returning to 4/4 as you play the **D** chord in the last bar on the word 'do'. You will recognise the solo riff in the tablature from the link between the chorus and the verse on the original recording.

Bsus2 Chord

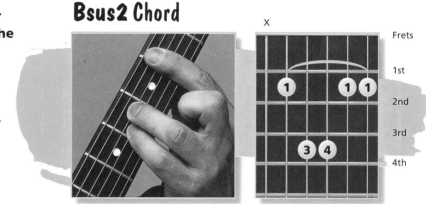

SOLO RIFF

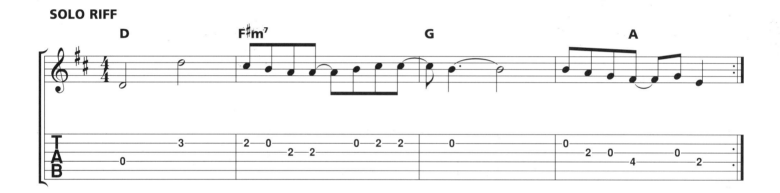

4 BAR INTRO

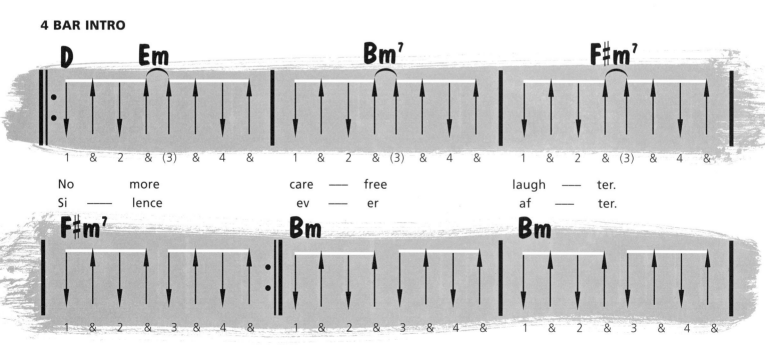

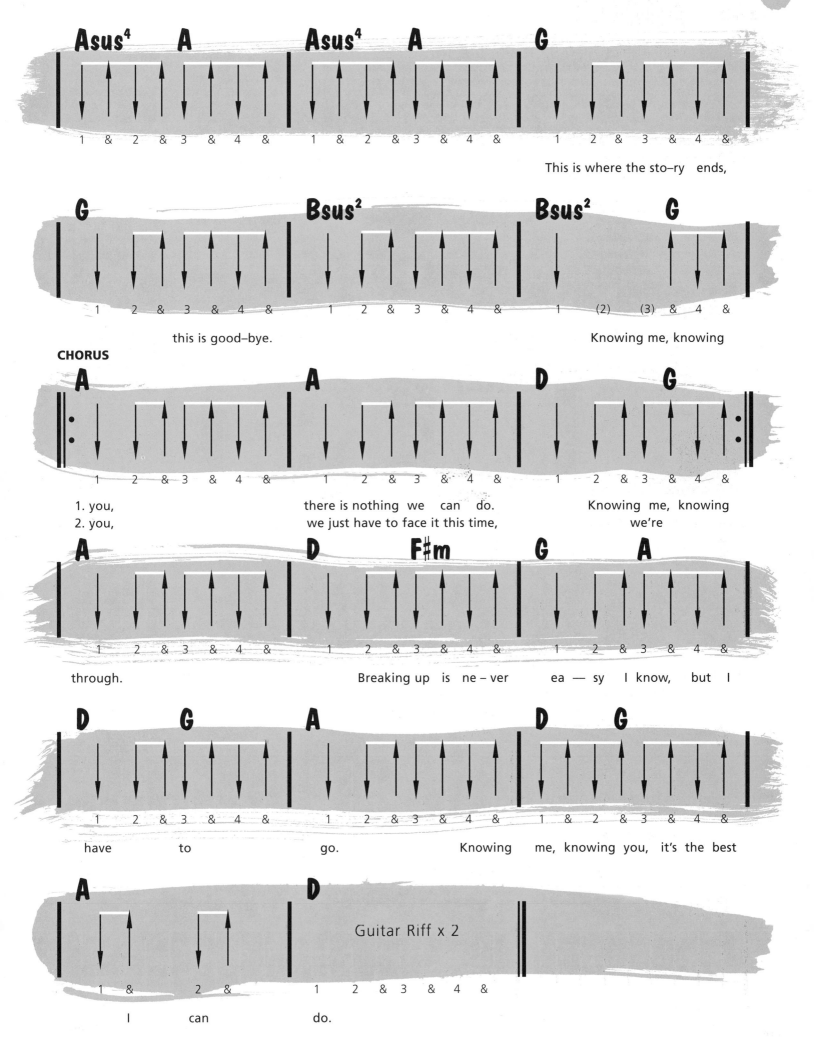

This is where the sto–ry ends,

this is good–bye.   Knowing me, knowing

CHORUS

1. you,   there is nothing we can do.   Knowing me, knowing
2. you,   we just have to face it this time,   we're

through.   Breaking up is ne – ver   ea — sy I know, but I

have   to   go.   Knowing   me, knowing you, it's the best

I   can   do.

ANGELS
Words & Music by Robbie Williams & Guy Chambers

Robbie Williams achieved huge chart success with this anthemic ballad, and we've provided the entire song this time.

This song has a slightly more complicated structure as a result. On the second time through you can either stick to our suggested strumming pattern, or continue the 'chorus' strumming pattern, as on the CD. Also, jump straight from bar 4 to bar 9, leaving out the bars in between.

The instruction 'Da Capo' at the end of the chorus means 'back to the beginning'. After the solo and chorus repeat, you finish there at the 'Fine' instruction.

The two new inversions below will complement the **G/B**, **C/E** and **D/F#** you already know. Remember that if you find inversions awkward you can always replace them with the ordinary root position version of the chord.

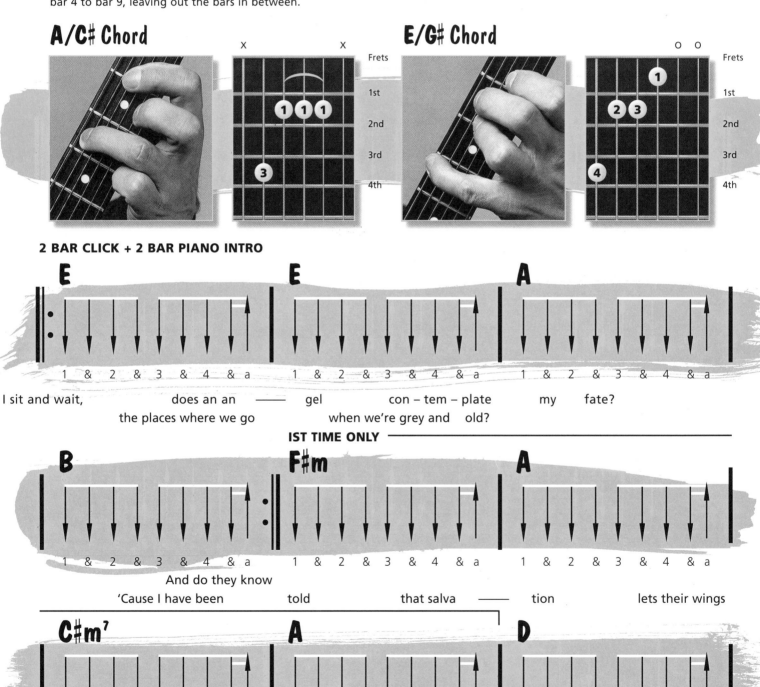

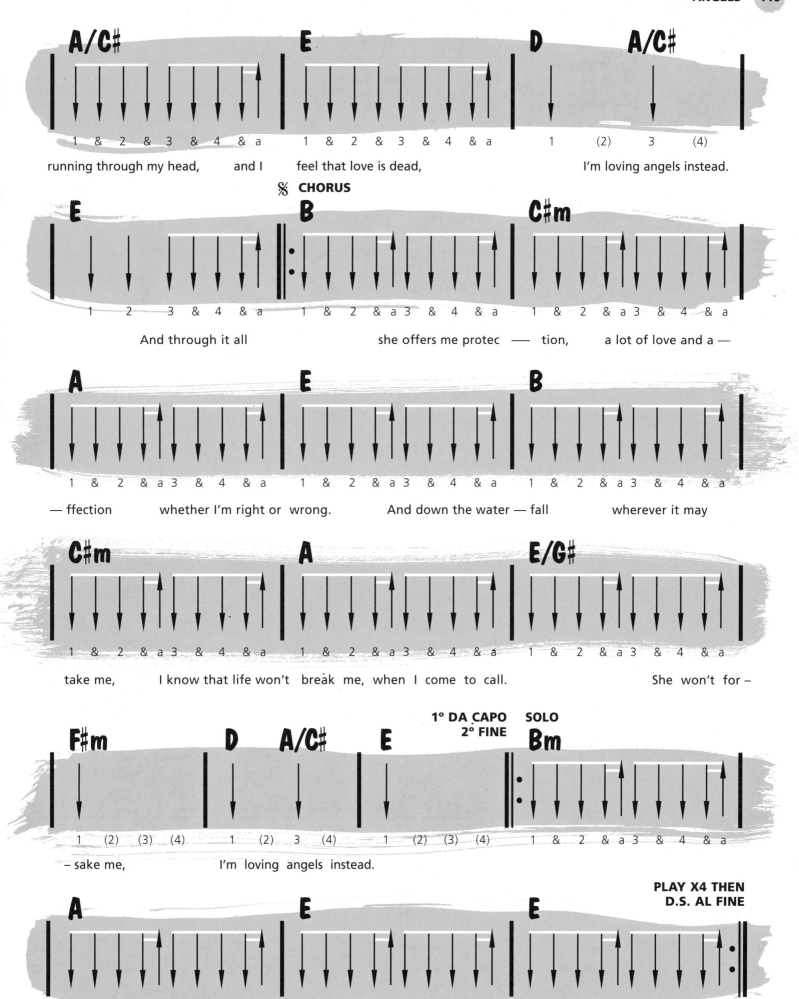

HERE COMES THE SUN
Words & Music by George Harrison

This much-loved ballad can be found on The Beatles' final album *Abbey Road*. It gets some of its 'sunny' quality from the high frequencies generated by the guitar which has a capo at the 7th fret.

The TAB is a bit more of a challenge. Here are the two arpeggio figures which occur at the end of the chorus and going into the bridge. These are good practice for accurate picking. Let the notes in each group ring out.

The chords are basic open shapes, with a simple strumming pattern. Watch out for the tricky timing in the bridge section - listen carefully to the CD to make sure you're getting it right.

George Harrison

GUITAR LINK (END OF CHORUS)

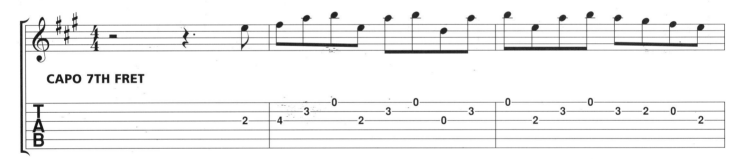

BRIDGE

CAPO 7TH FRET
3 BAR 'FADE-IN' INTRO
VERSE

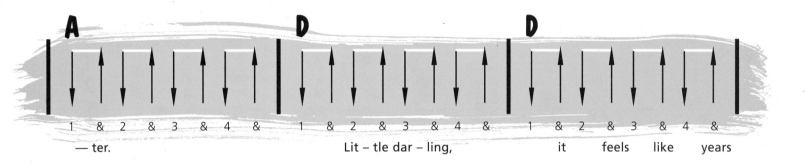

D — Lit – tle dar – ling,
D — it's been a long,
G — cold, lone —— ly win —

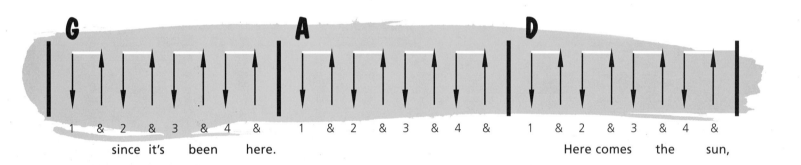

A — — ter.
D — Lit – tle dar – ling,
D — it feels like years

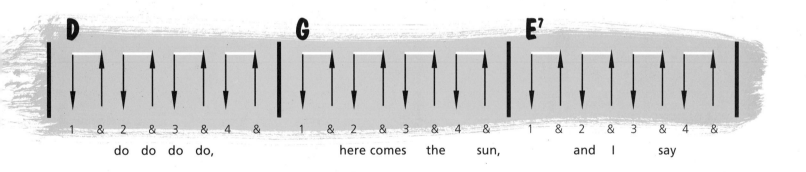

G — since it's been here.
A
D — Here comes the sun,

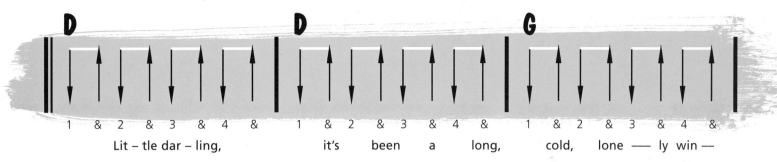

D — do do do do,
G — here comes the sun,
E⁷ — and I say

D — "It's all —— right."

Guitar Link   Guitar Link

Sting

EVERY BREATH YOU TAKE
Words & Music by Sting

'Every Breath You Take' is a love song with an undercurrent of menace, and was one of The Police's biggest hits on its release in 1983. To play along with the original recording, you will need to put a capo at the second fret to change the key from G major to A major.

Our tab arrangement gives you the basis of the song - all the lyrics are on page 133. We've also shown the chord shapes you'll need in order to play along. New to this song are **Gadd9**, **Aadd9**, **Cadd9** and **Emadd9**. All the rest should be familiar to you.

The **add9** chord is basically a major chord with the 'ninth' note of the scale added. Technically the ninth is also the second, so you can hear that it sounds a little like a suspended second.

While playing this part, you can either use thumb and fingers to play fingerstyle, or use a pick. A little muting with the picking hand will make it sound more like the original.

Gadd9 Chord

Aadd9 Chord

Cadd9 Chord

Emadd9 Chord

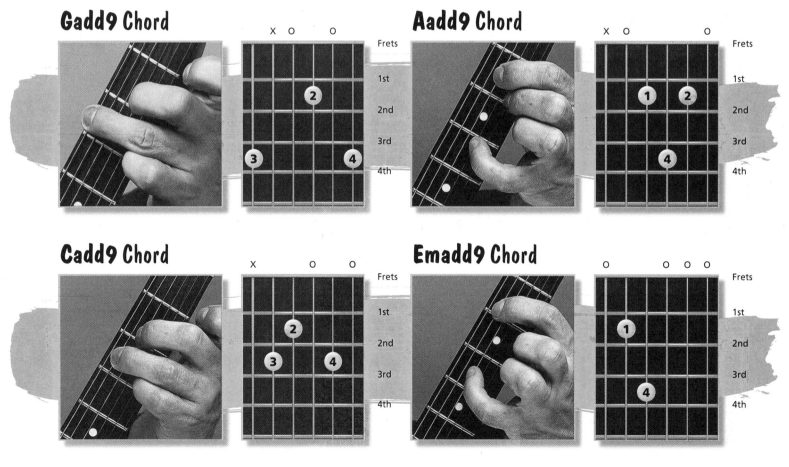

3 BAR 'FADE-IN' INTRO

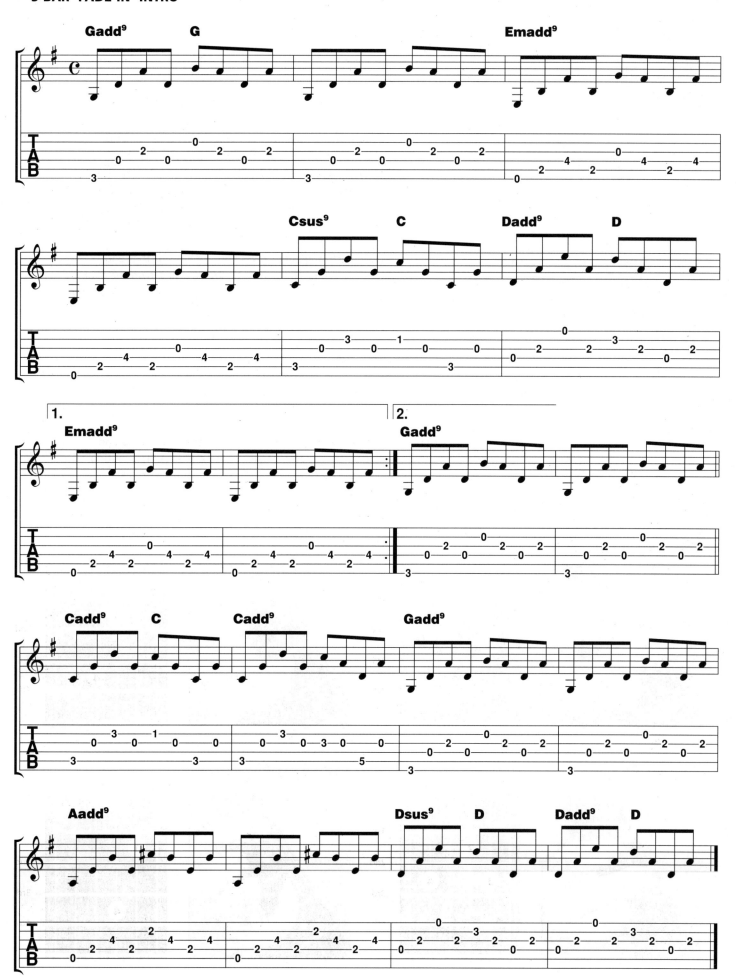

TEARS IN HEAVEN
Words & Music by Eric Clapton & Will Jennings

This touching ballad, played on acoustic guitar, comes from Eric Clapton's *Unplugged* album.

We've provided the TAB for the verse, chorus and bridge over the page - full lyrics are on page 134.
You might find the TAB part a bit of a challenge, so practise it in small sections. If you'd rather just strum along, there's an easy strumming part for the verse and chorus across the page, but for best results, try finger-picking the chords instead of just strumming them.

Once again, there are a few new chords that you'll need to learn, thanks to Eric's use of descending bass lines in this song! If you find the inversions confusing, then, as before, you can replace them with normal open chord shapes.
Tip: for any chord with /**E** or /**A**, just play the normal open chord and let the **E** or **A** string ring out below.

Eric Clapton

Esus4 Chord

C♯ Chord

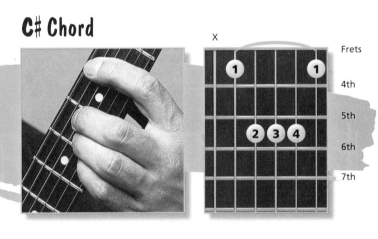

A7/E Chord

F♯7sus4 Chord

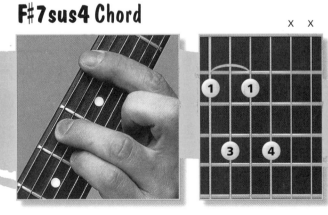

4 BAR 'FADE-IN' INTRO

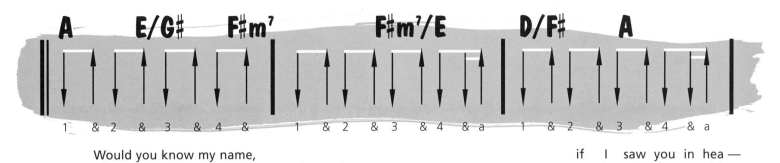

| A | E/G# | F#m⁷ | | F#m⁷/E | | D/F# | A |

Would you know my name,   if I saw you in hea —

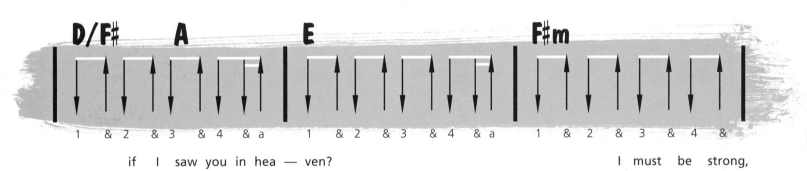

| E | | A | E/G# | F#m⁷ | | F#m⁷/E | |

— ven?   Would it be the same,

| D/F# | A | | E | | F#m | |

if I saw you in hea — ven?   I must be strong,

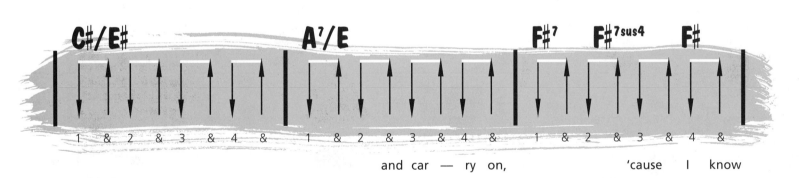

| C#/E# | | A⁷/E | | F#⁷ | F#⁷sus4 | F# |

and car — ry on,   'cause I know

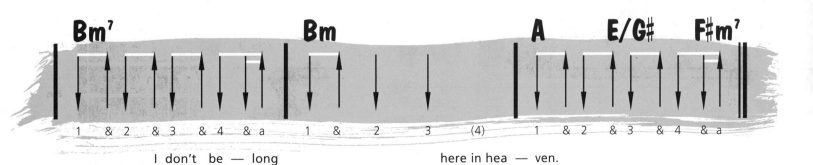

| Bm⁷ | | Bm | | A | E/G# | F#m⁷ |

I don't be — long   here in hea — ven.

4 BAR INTRO

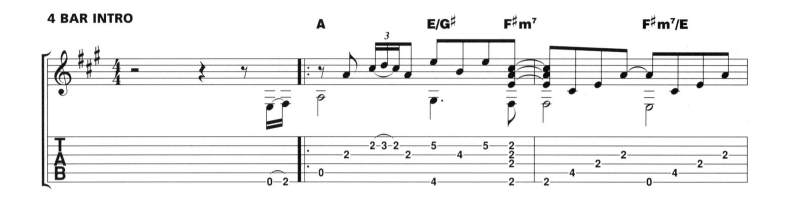

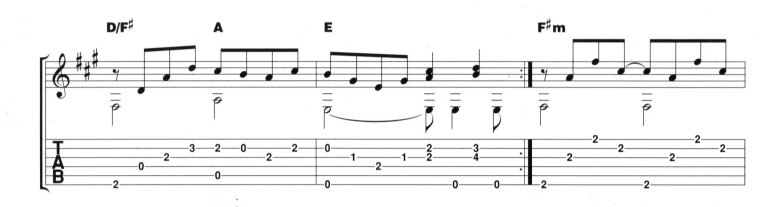

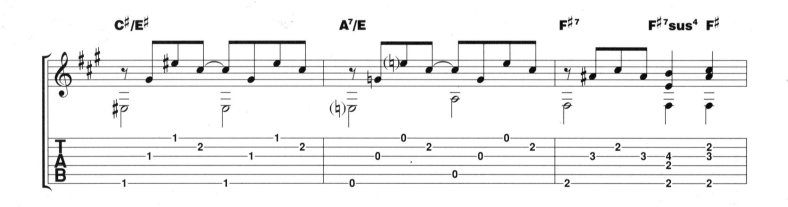

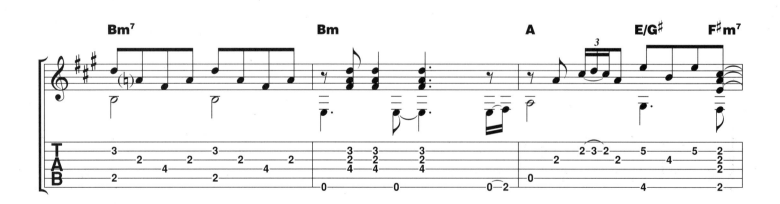

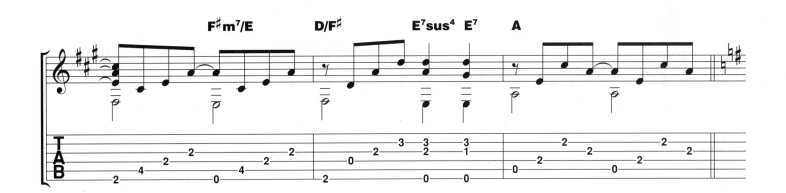

BRIDGE

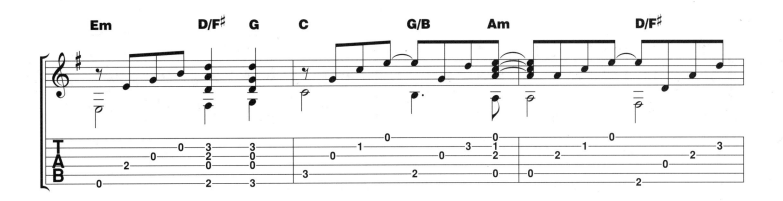

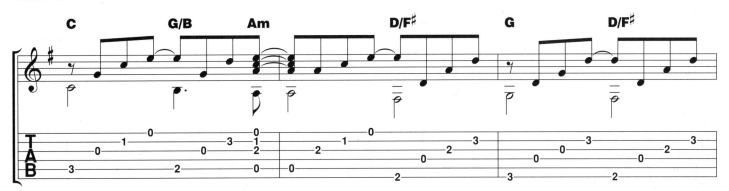

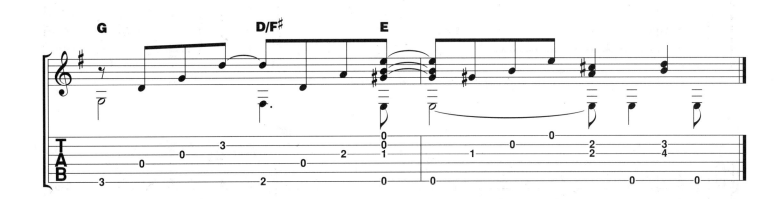

A DESIGN FOR LIFE

Words & Music by Nicky Wire, James Dean Bradfield & Sean Moore

This popular Manic Street Preachers track features a distinctive arpeggiated guitar part for the verse and chords for the chorus.

To play along with the CD, start across the page with the verse TAB part, then continue with the strumming pattern below, for the chorus.

For the TAB finger-picking part, play the bass note with your thumb and the other three notes with your 1st, 2nd and 3rd fingers in sequence. It is possible to play it just with a pick, but pick and fingers is easier.

Manic Street Preachers

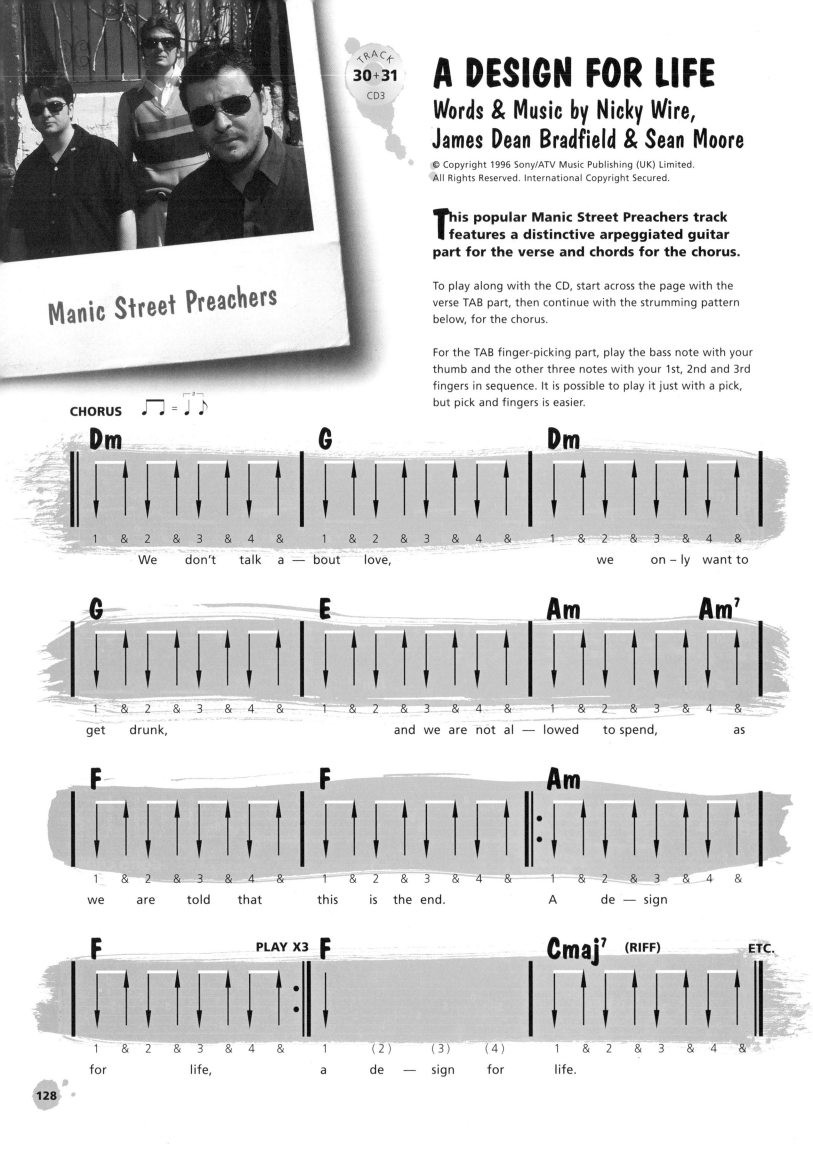

CHORUS

Dm / **G** / **Dm**

1 & 2 & 3 & 4 & | 1 & 2 & 3 & 4 & | 1 & 2 & 3 & 4 &

We don't talk a — bout love,   we on – ly want to

G / **E** / **Am** **Am⁷**

1 & 2 & 3 & 4 & | 1 & 2 & 3 & 4 & | 1 & 2 & 3 & 4 &

get drunk,   and we are not al — lowed to spend,   as

F / **F** / **Am**

1 & 2 & 3 & 4 & | 1 & 2 & 3 & 4 & | 1 & 2 & 3 & 4 &

we are told that this is the end.   A de — sign

F   PLAY X3 **F** / **Cmaj⁷** (RIFF)   ETC.

1 & 2 & 3 & 4 & | 1 (2) (3) (4) | 1 & 2 & 3 & 4 &

for life,   a de — sign for life.

2 BAR CLICK INTRO
VERSE: GUITAR PART

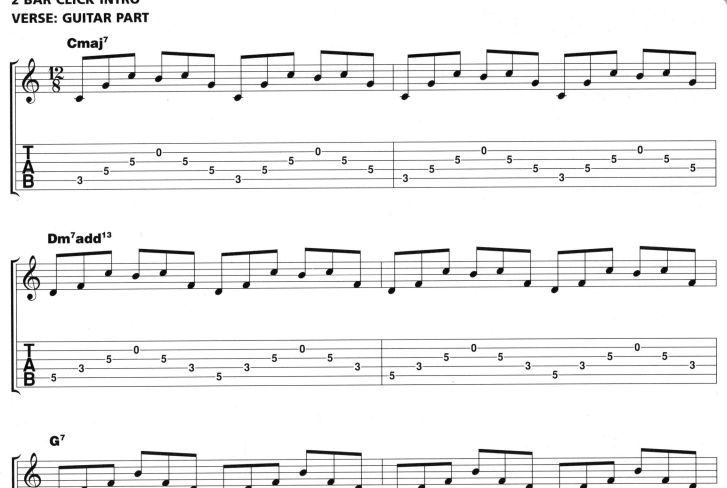

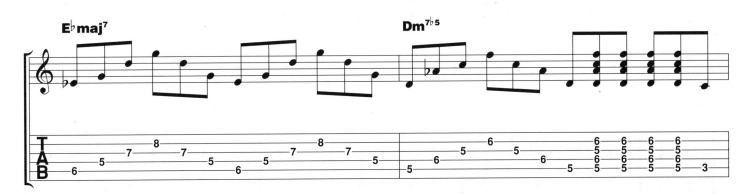

GO TO CHORUS
AFTER REPEAT

ADDITIONAL LYRICS

MRS ROBINSON

Intro
Di di di di di di di di di di di di di
Doo doo doo doo doo doo doo
doo doo
Di di di di di di di di di di di di di

Chorus
And here's to you, Mrs. Robinson
Jesus loves you more than you will
know (wo, wo, wo)
God bless you please, Mrs. Robinson
Heaven holds a place for those
who pray
(Hey, hey, hey... hey, hey, hey).

Verse 1
We'd like to know a little bit about
you for our files
We'd like to help you learn to help
yourself
Look around you, all you see are
sympathetic eyes
Stroll around the grounds until you
feel at home.

Chorus

Verse 2
Hide it in a hiding place where no one
ever goes
Put it in your pantry with your
cupcakes
It's a little secret, just the Robinsons'
affair
Most of all, you've got to hide it from
the kids.

Chorus

Verse 3
Sitting on a sofa on a Sunday
afternoon
Going to the candidates' debate
Laugh about it, shout about it
When you've got to choose.
Ev'ry way you look at it, you lose.

Chorus 2
Where have you gone, Joe DiMaggio?
A nation turns its lonely eyes to you
(woo, woo, woo)
What's that you say, Mrs. Robinson?
Joltin' Joe has left and gone away
(Hey, hey, hey... hey, hey, hey).

YELLOW

Verse 1
Look at the stars
Look how they shine for you
And everything you do
Yeah, they were all yellow.

I came alive
I wrote a song for you
And all the things you do
And it was yellow.
So then I took my turn
Oh, what a thing to've done
And it was all yellow.

Chorus
Your skin, oh yeah your skin
and bones
Turn into something beautiful
And you know, you know I love you so
You know I love you so.

Verse 2
I swam across
I jumped across for you
Oh, what a thing to do
'Cause you were all yellow.

I drew a line, I drew a line for you
Oh, what a thing to do
And it was all yellow.

Chorus 2
And your skin, oh yeah your skin and
bones
Turn into something beautiful
And you know for you I'd bleed
myself dry
For you I'd bleed myself dry.

Coda
It's true, look how they shine for you
Look how they shine for you
Look how they shine for
Look how they shine for you
Look how they shine for you
Look how they shine.

Look at the stars
Look how they shine for you
And all the things that you do.

A WHITER SHADE
OF PALE

Verse 1
We skipped the light fandango
Turned cartwheels 'cross the floor
I was feeling kind of seasick
The crowd called out for more
The room was humming harder
As the ceiling flew away
When we called out for another drink
The waiter brought a tray.

Chorus
And so it was that later
As the miller told his tale
That her face at first just ghostly
Turned a whiter shade of pale.

Verse 2
She said, "There is no reason
And the truth is plain to see"
But I wandered through my playing
cards
And would not let her be
One of sixteen vestal virgins
Who were leaving for the coast
And although my eyes were opened
They might just as well be closed

Chorus

LAYLA

Verse 1
What'll you do when you get lonely?
And no-body's waiting by your side
You been runnin' and hidin' much
too long
You know it's just your foolish pride.

Chorus
Layla, you got me on my knees
Layla, I'm beggin' darlin' please
Layla, darlin' won't you ease my
worried mind?

Verse 2
I tried to give you consolation
When your old man had let you down
Like a fool, I fell in love with you
You turned my whole world upside
down.

Chorus

Verse 3
Let's make the best of the situation
Before I finally go insane
Please don't say we'll never find a way
Don't tell me all my love's in vain.

Chorus to fade

(EVERYTHING I DO)
I DO IT FOR YOU

Verse 1
Look into my eyes, you will see
What you mean to me
Search your heart, search your soul
And when you find me there you'll
search no more
Don't tell me it's not worth trying for
You can't tell me it's not worth
dying for
You know it's true
Everything I do, I do it for you.

Verse 2
Look into your heart, and you will find
There's nothing there to hide
Take me as I am, take my life
I would give it all, I would sacrifice

Don't tell me it's not worth fighting
for
I can't help it, there's nothing I want
more
You know it's true
Everything I do, I do it for you.

Bridge
There's no love like your love
And no other could give more love
There's nowhere unless you're there
All the time, all the way.

Solo

Verse 3
Oh, you can't tell me it's not worth
trying for
I can't help it, there's nothing I want
more
Yeah, I would fight for you, I'd lie for
you
Walk the wire for you, yeah I'd die for
you
You know it's true
Everything I do
Oh I do it for you.

Coda (ad lib to fade)

MESSAGE IN A BOTTLE

Verse 1
Just a castaway, an island lost at sea-o
Another lonely day, no one here but
me-o
More loneliness than any man could
bear
Rescue me before I fall into despair-o.

Chorus
I'll send an S.O.S. to the world
I'll send an S.O.S. to the world
I hope that someone gets my
I hope that someone gets my
I hope that someone gets my
Message in a bottle, yeah.
Message in a bottle, yeah.

Verse 2
A year has passed since I wrote my
note
But I should have known this right
from the start
Only hope can keep me together
Love can mend your life but love can
break your heart.

Chorus

Message in a bottle, yeah.
Message in a bottle.

Verse 3
Walked out this morning I don't
believe what I saw
A hundred billion bottles washed up
on the shore
Seems I'm not alone in being alone
Hundred billion castaways looking for
a home.

Chorus

Message in a bottle, yeah.
Message in a bottle.

Coda (repeat to fade)
I'm sending out an S.O.S.

SULTANS OF SWING

Verse 1
You get a shiver in the dark, it's
raining in the park
But meantime, south of the river
You stop and you hold everything
A band is blowin' Dixie, double four
time
You feel all right when you hear the
music ring.

Verse 2
Well now you step inside
But you don't see too many faces
Comin' in out of the rain to hear the
jazz go down
Competition, in other places
But the horns, they're blowin' that
sound
Way on down south, way on down
south, London Town.

Verse 3
You check out Guitar George, he
knows all the chords
Mind he's strictly rhythm, he doesn't
want to make it cry or sing
This and an old guitar is all he can
afford
When he gets up under the lights to
play his thing.

Verse 4
And Harry doesn't mind if he doesn't
make the scene
He's got a daytime job, he's doin' all
right
He can play the honky-tonk like
anything
Savin' it up for Friday night
With the Sultans, with the Sultans of
Swing.

Verse 5
And the crowd of young boys
They're foolin' around in the corner
Drunk and dressed in their best brown
baggies and their platform soles
They don't give a damn about any
trumpet-playin' band
It ain't what they call rock 'n' roll
And the Sultans, yeah the Sultans,
they played Creole.

Instrumental

Verse 6
And then the man, he steps right up
to the microphone
And says, at last, just as the time-bell
rings:
"Good night now, it's time to go
home."
And he makes it fast with one more
thing:
"We are the Sultans, we are the
Sultans of Swing."

MULDER AND SCULLY

Verse 1
I'd rather be liberated, I find myself
captivated
Stop doing what you keep doing it too
I'd rather stay bold and lonely, I dream
I'm your one and only
Stop doing what you keep doing it
too.

Chorus
Things are getting strange, I'm starting
to worry
This could be a case for Mulder and
Scully
Things are getting strange, now I can't
sleep alone.

Verse 2
I'd rather be jumping ship, I find
myself jumping straight in
Stop doing what you keep doing it too
Forever be dozy and dim, I wake
myself thinking of him
Stop doing what you keep doing it
too.

Chorus

Bridge
My bed is made for two and there's
nothing I can do
So tell me something I don't know
If my head is full of you is there
nothing I can do?
Must we all march in two by two by
two?

Verse 3
And as for some happy ending
I'd rather stay single and thin
Stop doing what you keep doing to me

Chorus x 2

Coda
So what have you got to say about
that?
And what does someone do without
love?
And what does someone do with love?
And what have you got to say about
that?

GOODBYE YELLOW BRICK ROAD

Verse 1
When are you gonna come down
When are you gonna land?
I should have stayed on the farm
Should have listened to my old man.

You know you can't hold me forever
I didn't sign up with you
I'm not a present for your friends to
open
This boy's too young to be singing the
blues.

Chorus
So goodbye Yellow Brick Road
Where the dogs of society howl
You can't plant me in your penthouse
I'm going back to my plough
Back to the howling old owl in the
woods
Hunting the horny back toad
Oh I've finally decided my future lies
Beyond the Yellow Brick Road.

Verse 2
What do you think you'll do then
I bet that'll shoot down your plane
It'll take you a couple of vodka and
tonics
To set you on your feet again.

Maybe you'll get a replacement
There's plenty like me to be found
Mongrels who ain't got a penny
Sniffling for tidbits like you on the
ground.

Chorus

KNOWING ME, KNOWING YOU

Verse 1
No more carefree laughter
Silence ever after
Walking through an empty house
Tears in my eyes
This is where the story ends
This is goodbye.

Chorus
Knowing me, knowing you
There is nothing we can do
Knowing me, knowing you
We just have to face it
This time we're through
Breaking up is never easy I know
But I have to go
Knowing me, knowing you
It's the best I can do.

Verse 2
Memories, good days, bad days
They'll be with me always
In these old familiar rooms children
would play
Now there's only emptiness, nothing
to say.

Chorus x 2

ANGELS

Verse 1
I sit and wait
Does an angel contemplate my fate
And do they know
The places where we go
When we're grey and old?
'Cause I have been told
That salvation lets their wings unfold
So when I'm lying in my bed
Thoughts running through my head
And I feel that love is dead
I'm loving angels instead.

Chorus
And through it all
She offers me protection
A lot of love and affection
Whether I'm right or wrong
And down the waterfall
Wherever it may take me
I know that life won't break me
When I come to call
She won't forsake me
I'm loving angels instead.

Verse 2
When I'm feeling weak
And my pain walks down a one-way
street

I look above, and I know I'll always be
blessed with love
And as the feeling grows
She brings flesh to my bones
And when love is dead
I'm loving angels instead.

Chorus

Solo

Chorus

HERE COMES THE SUN

Chorus
Here comes the sun
Here comes the sun
And I say it's all right.

Verse 1
Little darling, it's been a long, cold,
lonely winter
Little darling, it feels like years since
it's been here.

Chorus

Verse 2
Little darling, the smile's returning to
their faces
Little darling, it seems like years since
it's been here.

Chorus

Bridge
Sun, sun, sun, here it comes
Sun, sun, sun, here it comes
Sun, sun, sun, here it comes
Sun, sun, sun, here it comes
Sun, sun, sun, here it comes

Verse 3
Little darling, I feel that ice is slowly
melting
Little darling, it seems like years since
it's been clear.

Chorus

Chorus

It's all right.

EVERY BREATH YOU TAKE

Verse 1
Every breath you take
Every move you make
Every bond you break
Every step you take
I'll be watching you.

Verse 2
Every single day
Every word you say
Every game you play
Every night you stay
I'll be watching you.

Bridge
Oh can't you see you belong to me
How my poor heart aches with every
step you take.

Verse 3
Every move you make
Every vow you break
Every smile you fake
Every claim you stake
I'll be watching you.

Middle
Since you've been gone I've been lost
without a trace
I dream at night I can only see your
face
I look around but it's you I can't
replace
I feel so cold and I long for your
embrace
I keep crying baby, baby, please.

Repeat Bridge

Repeat Verse 3

Coda
Every move you make
Every step you take
I'll be watching you
I'll be watching you
I'll be watching you.

Repeat to fade

TEARS IN HEAVEN

Verse 1

Would you know my name
If I saw you in heaven?
Would it be the same
If I saw you in heaven?

Chorus 1

I must be strong and carry on
'Cause I know I don't belong
Here in heaven.

Verse 2

Would you hold my hand
If I saw you in heaven?
Would you help me stand
If I saw you in heaven?

Chorus 2

I'll find my way through night and day
'Cause I know I just can't stay
Here in heaven.

Bridge

Time can bring you down
Time can bend your knees
Time can break your heart
Have you beggin' please
Beggin' please.

Solo

Chorus 3

Beyond the door there's peace
I'm sure
And I know there'll be no more
Tears in heaven.

Verse 3

Would you know my name
If I saw you in heaven?
Would you be the same
If I saw you in heaven?

Repeat Chorus 1

Coda

'Cause I know I don't belong
Here in heaven.

A DESIGN FOR LIFE

Verse 1

Libraries gave us power
Then work came and made us free
What price now
For a shallow piece of dignity?

Verse 2

I wish I had a bottle
Right here in my dirty face
To wear the scars
To show from where I came.

Chorus

We don't talk about love
We only want to get drunk
And we are not allowed to spend
As we are told that this is the end
A design for life, a design for life
A design for life, a design for life.

Verse 3

I wish I had a bottle
Right here in my pretty face
To wear the scars
To show from where I came.

Chorus x 2

Printed in Malta by Progress Press Co. Ltd   12/06 (60683)

The Complete Rock & Pop Guitar Player

CONCLUSION

Congratulations! Now you have worked your way through the three parts of *The Complete Rock & Pop Guitar Player* you are ready to explore the world of guitar playing in more depth.

• If you want to do more chord strumming check out the many titles in the popular *Chord Songbook* series.

• If you want to learn well-known songs and albums in more detail look for a band/artist matching folio which will show you solos and riffs note for note, or try the excellent *Play Guitar With...* series.

• If you want to improve your lead guitar playing, your ability to improvise, or delve into the wonderful world of altered tunings, have a look at the *FastForward* series. All *FastForward* books are equipped with a CD so you can hear the examples and play along.

CD 1

1 **Tuning Notes**

2 **Paperback Writer** (Lennon / McCartney)
Northern Songs / Sony / ATV Music
Publishing (UK) Limited

3 **Paperback Writer** Backing track only

4 **Brimful Of Asha** (Singh)
Universal / Momentum Music Limited

5 **Brimful Of Asha** Backing track only

6 **Hello, I Love You**
(Morrison / Krieger / Manzarek / Densmore)
Rondor Music (London) Limited

7 **Hello, I Love You** Backing track only

8 **Rock Around The Clock**
(Freedman / De Knight)
Myers Music Limited

9 **Rock Around The Clock**
Backing track only

10 **That'll Be The Day**
(Holly / Petty / Allison)
Peermusic (UK) Limited

11 **That'll Be The Day** Backing track only

12 **I Wanna Be Adored** (Squire / Brown)
Zomba Music Publishers Limited

13 **I Wanna Be Adored** Backing track only

14 **Stand By Me** (King / Leiber / Stoller)
Hornall Brothers Music Limited

15 **Stand By Me** Backing track only

16 **Cathy's Clown** (Everly)
Acuff-Rose Music Limited

17 **Cathy's Clown** Backing track only

18 **Common People** (Cocker / Pulp)
Universal / Island Music Limited

19 **Common People** Backing track only

20 **All Along The Watchtower** (Dylan)
Sony / ATV Music Publishing (UK) Limited

21 **All Along The Watchtower**
Backing track only

22 **No Woman, No Cry** (Ford)
Blue Mountain Music Limited

23 **No Woman, No Cry** Backing track only

24 **Dance Away** (Ferry)
BMG Songs Limited

25 **Dance Away** Backing track only

26 **That's Entertainment** (Weller)
BMG Music Publishing Limited

27 **That's Entertainment**
Backing track only

28 **Sit Down**
(Booth / Gott / Whelan / Glennie)
Blue Mountain Music Limited

29 **Sit Down** Backing track only

30 **So Far Away** (Knopfler)
Rondor Music (London) Limited

31 **So Far Away** Backing track only

32 **Half The World Away** (Gallagher)
Sony / ATV Music Publishing (UK) Limited

33 **Half The World Away**
Backing track only

34 **American Pie** (McLean)
Universal / MCA Music Limited

35 **American Pie** Backing track only

CD 2

1 **Tuning Notes**

2 **Blue Suede Shoes** (Perkins)
Carlin Music Corporation

3 **Blue Suede Shoes** Backing track only

4 **Driftwood** (Healy)
Sony / ATV Music Publishing (UK) Limited

5 **Driftwood** Backing track only

6 **Sail Away** (Gray)
Chrysalis Music Limited

7 **Sail Away** Backing track only

8 **Wild Wood** (Weller)
Notting Hill Music (UK) Limited

9 **Wild Wood** Backing track only

10 **Roll With It** (Gallagher)
Sony / ATV Music Publishing (UK) Limited

11 **Roll With It** Backing track only

12 **20th Century Boy** (Bolan)
Wizard (Bahamas) Limited

13 **20th Century Boy**
Backing track only

14 **She Loves You** (Lennon / McCartney)
Northern Songs / Sony /
ATV Music Publishing (UK) Limited

15 **She Loves You** Backing track only

16 **I Shot The Sheriff** (Marley)
Blue Mountain Music Limited

17 **I Shot The Sheriff** Backing track only

18 **Sunny Afternoon** (Davies)
Carlin Music Corporation

19 **Sunny Afternoon** Backing track only

20 **There She Goes** (Mavers)
Universal / Island Music Limited

21 **There She Goes** Backing track only

22 **Hey Joe** (Roberts)
Carlin Music Corporation

23 **Hey Joe** Backing track only

24 **All Right Now** (Rodgers / Fraser)
Blue Mountain Music Limited

25 **All Right Now** Backing track only

26 **Nights In White Satin** (Hayward)
Tyler Music Limited

27 **Nights In White Satin**
Backing track only

28 **While My Guitar Gently Weeps**
(Harrison) Harrisongs Limited

29 **While My Guitar Gently Weeps**
Backing track only

30 **Pinball Wizard** (Townshend)
Fabulous Music Limited

31 **Pinball Wizard** Backing track only

32 **Light My Fire**
(Morrison / Krieger / Manzarek / Densmore)
Rondor Music (London) Limited

33 **Light My Fire** Backing track only

See inside front cover for CD 1, and
inside back cover for CD 2 & CD 3.

To remove a CD from its plastic sleeve,
lift the small lip on the side to break the
perforated flap. Replace the disc after use
for convenient storage.

CD 3

1 **Tuning Notes**

2 **Mrs. Robinson** (Simon)
Pattern Music

3 **Mrs. Robinson** Backing track only

4 **Yellow**
(Berryman / Buckland / Champion / Martin)
BMG Music Publishing Limited

5 **Yellow** Backing track only

6 **A Whiter Shade Of Pale**
(Reid / Brooker)
Onward Music Limited

7 **A Whiter Shade Of Pale**
Backing track only

8 **Layla** (Clapton / Gordon)
Warner Chappell Music Limited

9 **Layla** Backing track only

10 **(Everything I Do) I Do It For You**
(Adams / Lange / Kamen)
Universal / MCA Music Limited /
Rondor Music (London) Limited /
Zomba Music Publishers Ltd

11 **(Everything I Do) I Do It For You**
Backing track only

12 **Message In A Bottle** (Sting)
Magnetic Publishing Limited / EMI Music
Publishing Limited

13 **Message In A Bottle** Backing track only

14 **Sultans Of Swing** (Knopfler)
Rondor Music (London) Limited

15 **Sultans Of Swing** Backing track only

16 **Mulder And Scully** (Matthews /
Roberts / Richards / Jones / Powell)
Sony / ATV Music Publishing (UK) Limited

17 **Mulder And Scully** Backing track only

18 **Goodbye Yellow Brick Road**
(John / Taupin)
Universal/Dick James Music Limited

19 **Goodbye Yellow Brick Road**
Backing track only

20 **Knowing Me, Knowing You**
(Andersson / Ulvaeus / Anderson)
Bocu Music Limited

21 **Knowing Me, Knowing You**
Backing track only

22 **Angels** (Williams / Chambers)
EMI Virgin Music Limited /
BMG Music Publishing Limited

23 **Angels** Backing track only

24 **Here Comes The Sun** (Harrison)
Harrisongs Limited

25 **Here Comes The Sun**
Backing track only

26 **Every Breath You Take** (Sting)
Magnetic Publishing Limited /
EMI Music Publishing Limited

27 **Every Breath You Take**
Backing track only

28 **Tears In Heaven** (Clapton / Jennings)
Warner Chappell Music Limited /
Rondor Music (London) Limited

29 **Tears In Heaven** Backing track only

30 **A Design For Life**
(Wire / Bradfield / Moore)
Sony / ATV Music Publishing (UK) Limited

31 **A Design For Life** Backing track only